PRAISE FOR
WHAT WHITE PARENTS SHO___ ABOUT TRANSRACIAL ADOPTION—THE WORKBOOK

"This is such a necessary resource despite the uniqueness of every adoption and every adoptee. I commend Melissa for taking the painstaking effort to help parents navigate what could be on the horizon and, more importantly, to validate adoptee perspectives and experiences!"

—Michelle Li, journalist, Korean adoptee, and co-founder of The Very Asian Foundation

". . . a must-have for all adoption practitioners and agencies! Melissa has struck gold again in putting this workbook together. Her incredible insight and keen perception into the challenges of transracial adoption shine through every page. . . . Prospective adoptive parents will find a concise and well-thought-out map to navigating adoptive parenting in a way that is child centered and elevates the adoptee experience. Get it, learn from it, and be the best adoptive parent you can be."

—Ruth dos Santos, co-creator of The Adoption Companion

". . . a powerful workbook that will help adoptive parents support and understand their child. Melissa has gone above and beyond to make sure any parent that goes through this workbook is equipped with the right language, knowledge, and action steps to be a great parent. I would suggest this to any transracial adoptive parent as an essential part of their parenting journey."

—Isaac Etter, founder of Identity

"I feel like the questions and personal stories made me truly open my eyes and self-reflect into the reasons why I adopted and if I'm doing the work to do right by my adoptee. As a Black transracial adoptive parent, I think *all* adoptive parents could benefit from this book!"

—Jeena Wilder, adoptive mom and creator of Hey There Wilders

"In this thought-provoking workbook amplifying the experiences of adoptees, the reader learns that white adoptive parents cannot support the children they choose to adopt without vulnerably examining their own positionality on race, adoption, and systems of power—none of which are mutually exclusive. A must-have for anyone seeking to support adoptees of color."

—Dr. Tony Hynes, adoptee and author of *The Son with Two Moms*

"... a comprehensive guide to the tough topics that every transracial/transnational family will face over the course of time and how to compassionately navigate them. This workbook will be a staple for families and adoption professionals worldwide."

—Jessica M. Luciere, transracial adoptee, adoptee advocate, and manager of community engagements and post-adoption services at Spence-Chapin

"Melissa has done it again: asking you direct questions to get to the heart of the issue. For adopted children to have the best possible outcomes, adoptive parents need to heed adult adoptee voices like Melissa's."

—Haley Radke, adoptee and creator of the *Adoptees On* podcast

"Fifteen years ago when I started the adoption process, my narrative around adoption was limited to an understanding as seen through the adoptive parent lens. As my family grew through adoption, my understanding of the adoption narrative grew as well. More recently, as social media has grown and adult adoptees have boldly and generously shared their stories, my understanding of the adoption narrative has shifted tremendously. [This workbook] created by Melissa Guida-Richards is the tool I didn't know I needed all those years ago. It is a treasure for an adoptive parent. The gold within its pages will bend and stretch you, in all the right ways, if you will allow it. And I hope you will."

—Heather Avis, *New York Times* best-selling author

WHAT WHITE PARENTS SHOULD KNOW ABOUT TRANSRACIAL ADOPTION

THE WORKBOOK

WHAT WHITE PARENTS SHOULD KNOW ABOUT TRANSRACIAL ADOPTION

THE WORKBOOK

PRACTICAL TOOLS, SKILLS, AND PROMPTS FOR AFFIRMING YOUR ADOPTED CHILD'S CULTURAL IDENTITY

MELISSA GUIDA-RICHARDS

Foreword and therapeutic supplements by
Marcella Moslow, LCSW, RPT

North Atlantic Books
Huichin, unceded Ohlone land
Berkeley, California

Published by
North Atlantic Books
Huichin, unceded Ohlone land
Berkeley, California

Cover art © chrupka via Getty Images
Cover design by Jasmine Hromjak
Book design by Happenstance Type-O-Rama

Printed in the United States of America

What White Parents Should Know about Transracial Adoption—The Workbook: Practical Tools, Skills, and Prompts for Affirming Your Adopted Child's Cultural Identity is sponsored and published by North Atlantic Books, an educational nonprofit based in the unceded Ohlone land Huichin (Berkeley, CA) that collaborates with partners to develop cross-cultural perspectives; nurture holistic views of art, science, the humanities, and healing; and seed personal and global transformation by publishing work on the relationship of body, spirit, and nature.

North Atlantic Books's publications are distributed to the US trade and internationally by Penguin Random House Publisher Services. For further information, visit our website at www.northatlanticbooks.com.

Library of Congress Cataloging-in-Publication Data

Names: Guida-Richards, Melissa, 1993- author.
Title: What white parents should know about transracial adoption: the
    workbook : practical tools, skills, and prompts for affirming your
    adopted child's cultural identity / Melissa Guida-Richards ; foreword
    and therapeutic supplements by Marcella Moslow, LCSW, RPT.
Description: Berkeley, California : North Atlantic Books, [2023] | Includes
    bibliographical references and index. | Summary: "This practical
    workbook guides readers to better understand transracial adoption and do
    the work of anti-racist, trauma-informed parenting by offering a wealth
    of activities, templates, and questions for self-reflection"-- Provided
    by publisher.
Identifiers: LCCN 2022051185 (print) | LCCN 2022051186 (ebook) | ISBN
    9781623178710 (trade paperback) | ISBN 9781623178727 (ebook)
Subjects: LCSH: Interracial adoption. | Intercountry adoption. | Adoptive
    parents. | Adopted children--Psychology. | Ethnicity in children. | Race
    awareness.
Classification: LCC HV875.6 .G85 2023 (print) | LCC HV875.6 (ebook) | DDC
    362.734089--dc23
LC record available at https://lccn.loc.gov/2022051185
LC ebook record available at https://lccn.loc.gov/2022051186

1 2 3 4 5 6 7 8 9 VERSA 28 27 26 25 24 23

North Atlantic Books is committed to the protection of our environment. We print on recycled paper whenever possible and partner with printers who strive to use environmentally responsible practices.

*For all the transracial adoptees and
foster youth in the world who deserve
parents who embrace their culture and
recognize the complexity of adoption.*

CONTENTS

FOREWORD

About a year ago I came across a book entitled *What White Parents Should Know about Transracial Adoption*. It immediately caught my eye, not only because of its bright orange cover, but also because of the directness of the title that was directly applicable to me/my family and so many families I work with. I was also thrilled to see that it was written by a fellow transracial adoptee. Adoptee voices bring so much value to the adoption arena and can provide insight and expertise that others cannot. After reading it, I reached out to Melissa to thank her for her work, as it is now an added resource I can recommend to families within my practice. It is one of many tools adoptive families can utilize to promote healthy, open, and trauma-informed relationships. I was honored when Melissa connected with me about helping with this workbook and am hopeful that it will support many families along their journey.

I cannot recall a time when I did not know the word *adoption* or that it somehow applied to me. It has been part of my narrative for as long as I can remember, going all the way back to the beginning. *Transracial*, on the other hand, was a word I was not exposed to until graduate school, and I never put the two words together as a way to identify myself until my mid-twenties (well past the identity stage of development!). Growing up, I never identified as a different race, yet somehow I knew I wasn't the same as everyone else. I knew I was Colombian—that's why my skin and features were darker—but I knew nothing beyond that, and I had no insight into what I would be subjected to because of it. I was never given the language to define myself or my family, and I was never immersed in what being Colombian truly meant. As I reflect, I can see how my experience isn't unique; over the years, I have encountered so many adoptive families that place the focus on their child being adopted, as opposed to their child being a transracial adoptee. They give space for some parts of our identity, but not all.

The adoption portion of this term is so often celebrated that it becomes part of an individual's identity. Yet somehow the trauma and racial aspects associated with transracial adoption are hidden in the shadows, often unacknowledged until an issue occurs. For me the meaning and significance of those words has shifted and changed over time, and I now identify as a transracial adoptee. I make space for both parts of this term. I find the need to put the transracial aspect first because my race is undeniably what people see about me first, especially when I am in the vicinity of my adoptive family. The narrative and the language have changed because I was, and still am, open to learning and growing. I'm committed to doing the work and I have made space for the complexities of my story, honoring all parts.

Through the process of my healing, I began to broach difficult and necessary conversations with my adoptive parents/family who had not done the work to the extent they probably needed to. For me, doing my own work opened the door for those close to me to start doing the same. It is my hope that through resources like the one you are holding, the onus will no longer fall on the adoptee to get the ball rolling in order to get what they need. It is my greatest hope that by doing your own inner and outer work, you as an adoptive parent/caregiver can take some of the burden from the child you have adopted/plan to adopt to keep from piling more complex trauma on their shoulders.

I was adopted as a six-week-old infant from Bogota, Colombia, by a white family from Buffalo, New York. Two and a half years later, my brother was also transracially adopted. Throughout my life we maintained close ties to Colombia, the people we knew there, and the network of families within the Buffalo area who had also adopted children transracially/transnationally through the same foundation. Throughout my childhood *adoption* was associated with words like *family*, *love*, *FANA* (the foundation at which my brother and I were placed in Colombia), and *friends*. However, there was minimal conversation about the immense losses and challenges of adoption and even less about the differences between our racial backgrounds and those of our peers and what that would look like for us as we grew older. We were essentially raised as white kids.

Looking back on it now, I both see and feel the absence of space for anything other than the joyful components of adoption. I was given no room to express the frustration of having to explain how I was related to all the white people. No room to grieve the loss not only of my biological family members but an entire birth country and culture. No room to communicate my anger regarding my lack of validation and control and the overall absence of emotional attunement I felt from my parents. No room to process the confusion I endured that came from trying to sort out all of my unprocessed feelings, thoughts, and sensations that remained undigested in my mind, heart, and body. Space was only made for a fraction of my experience, and this came with a price.

That price was disconnection—a feeling of being misunderstood by the people I was supposed to be the closest to. I faced the challenge of knowing that not only could my parents not fully comprehend what it was like to be adopted, but also, on top of that, they could not help me navigate any racial issues that I inevitably did (and still do) face.

I understand that this is perplexing to many because my parents did many things that were right on point. That being said, it was still not enough. The pre-adoption education they received was by no means comprehensive or integrative, and the reality is, as two white individuals, they did not have any experience with being on the receiving end of racism in this country. Due to that, their approach was less than trauma informed, and they were underequipped to parent children with developmental trauma who were also of a different race.

I believe wholeheartedly that they did the best they could with what they were given at the time. However, the reality is that now we know more, and therefore ongoing work is not optional. In fact, it never should have been optional. It is my stance that adoptive parents have a responsibility to be on a continuous journey of learning to best support their child mentally, emotionally, and physically. This is how we make adoption truly adoptee centric. My parents' lack of understanding and attunement caused me to feel disconnected from them; I also felt a great deal of pain, even though I know they never intended to cause me harm. After experiencing this throughout my childhood and young adulthood (and still, sometimes, to this day), I became committed to helping other adoptees and their families who find themselves in these circumstances and to elevating the voices of adoptees, who are the true experts due to our lived experience.

As I grew into adulthood, I emersed myself in learning about topics like trauma, attachment, dissociation, the nervous system, trauma responses, trauma-informed care, and more. I engaged in and became trained and certified in modalities that take neurobiology, and the impacts of trauma on the brain and body, into account—those that acknowledge that trauma starts in utero and those that, ultimately, can help heal the wounds that traumatic experiences inflict. It all started to click and I finally had information to back up the silent thoughts and feelings I had carried throughout my life.

The information that I started to share really rocked the boat for many in my personal and professional worlds, and I was met with a great deal of resistance and cognitive dissonance, which added complexity to my own traumatic experiences. Societally, people are still quick to jump on the bandwagon that adoption is beautiful, that love can see through color, that it is a seamless adjustment, and that there is little to no space for acknowledging any potential challenges to or downfalls of this system. Despite these reactions, I was determined to provide services and resources for adoptees of all ages, for their families, and for the professionals who work with this population who could be truly adoptee focused. I knew the need was there.

The reality is that adoptive families, no matter what stage they are in process, are in desperate need of help. Adoptees in general are struggling immensely and are a marginalized population that is rarely spoken about. Adoptees are overrepresented in hospitals, prisons, mental health treatment centers, and more. Specifically, transracial adoptees continue to navigate the harsh realities of being Black and Brown in the United States, and they grapple with the fact that their adoptive parents' whiteness will not help them in the real world. Adoptive parents/caregivers don't understand the complexities or how to help. Adoptive parents have also been let down and done a disservice by the adoption industry because there are huge gaps in the education it provides. The critical education adoptive parents require to effectively parent children with these specific needs is overlooked, denied, or withheld. I witness a tangible helplessness within family systems that stems from this lack of education, acceptance, and acknowledgment of core issues, from the absence of validation, and from overall misunderstanding, all of which rupture connections within the family. This is the biggest barrier to healing; without connection these adoptees and their families have no chance of healing.

Adoptive parents are often at their wits' end, filled with feelings of powerlessness and overwhelm; most say they have tried everything and the situation feels like it's getting worse. I advise adoptive parents I know and work with that they must come to a space in which they can accept that their child has special needs; they must educate themselves and allow this new knowledge to be the foundation on which they base their trauma-informed parenting throughout their child's life. For families of transracial adoptees, being racially informed and anti-racist are integral parts of being trauma informed. Many adoptive families experience the stigma of feeling like they are the only ones facing challenges because trauma related to transracial adoption is assumed not to be real or isn't talked about. It is because of stigmas like this that I have seen so many families, including my own, struggle in silence.

Thankfully, I have started to see small shifts during my years in the field. Little by little, more adoptive parents are finally ready to pursue the possibility that some of what is going on between them and their children may be related to early trauma. Within my clinical practice, adoptive parents find themselves reaching out when they realize they are stuck. Their children present with depression or anxiety, have trouble building and maintaining relationships, self-harm, have emotional and behavioral dysregulation, or abuse substances—all stemming from deeper wounds and layers of complex trauma. Themes of grief, rejection, abandonment, loss, identity, and shame are all too common throughout my practice.

For those of my clients who were adopted transracially, I find that their white adoptive parents also need help—help incorporating and honoring their child's birth culture, help addressing racism and biases within their adoptive family, help navigating how to assist their child in connecting with their birth country, help figuring out what actions they need to take to promote healthy identity formation, and help identifying parent trauma versus adoptee trauma and how they can trigger each other. These parents find that the education their agencies provided does/did not offer real-world deep dives into these areas. In my opinion, this lack of education perpetuates a belief that I see commonly among adoptive parents, both personally and professionally—that adoptive parents can get away with doing the bare minimum and everything will be fine. Nothing could be further from the truth.

My message to you as you dive into this workbook: This is just one step of many. I encourage you to be open and willing to engage in the lifelong journey alongside the transracial adoptee in your life. Finding a way to protect, embrace, and honor all parts of them is part of your work on this journey. It will require you to tolerate what is uncomfortable and to learn from those with lived experience instead of relying on an inaccurate societal narrative that gets spoon fed to you by the adoption industry. There is no concrete end point or age at which an adoptee will "graduate" from having these needs or when these themes will vanish. You're signing up for a lifelong commitment, so pace yourselves. This is a marathon, not a sprint. Putting in the emotional effort by using workbooks like this, in addition to reading, engaging in therapy, listening to podcasts, and interacting with other adoptees and individuals outside of your race creates an opportunity for maximum integration for your family system.

Also, please know it is never too early or too late to start this journey. Parts of me wish my adoptive parents committed to this sooner. Although earlier action on their part would not have made things perfect, it could have significantly changed the dynamics within our family and better met my needs. That being said, I am so glad that their perspectives have shifted and that now they choose to be more open, to learn, and to have the hard conversations that rested silently between us for so many years. It has brought our family closer and to a place of greater respect and understanding, and I see the same transformation happen with the families I work with.

I know it sounds daunting, and at times it definitely will be, but please keep in mind, doing right by your child means doing the work.

I wish you all the best on your journey,

MARCELLA MOSLOW
Transracial and transnational adoptee
LCSW, RPT

INTRODUCTION

Dear Adoptive Parent,

My name is Melissa Guida-Richards and I am a transracial and late-discovery adoptee who was adopted internationally from Bogotá, Colombia, when I was about five months old. Some of you may know me as the author of the companion book to this workbook, *What White Parents Should Know about Transracial Adoption* (which I'll sometimes refer to as *WWPSKATA*), but for those of you who are unfamiliar with my work, I'll share a little bit more about me.

In 2019, I had a big break when my *HuffPost* article "My Adoptive Parents Hid My Racial Identity from Me for 19 Years" went viral. Since then I've had articles published in the *New York Times*, *Insider*, the *Independent*, *HuffPost*, and more; I've been on panels with Amazon and *Good Day LA*; and I've taken part in workshops with many adoption agencies in the US and overseas. In my spare time, I am the creator and founder of the *Adoptee Thoughts* Instagram page and podcast, where I raise the voices of adoptees and share about the nuances in adoption.

The purpose of my work, and, in turn, this workbook, is to provide the adoption community with resources that center adoptee voices and that help prepare adoptive parents for the journey on which they are about to embark. Although you may find some of the topics I cover difficult to read about at first (e.g., white saviorism, white fragility, toxic positivity), I hope you find that the questions and activities I provide in this workbook foster deeper thought and conversation about adoption.

Adoption is often thought to be about saving a child in need, but it is much more complex than that. Different factors go into placing a child, the adoption industry has systemic issues, and some parents getting ready to adopt have a variety of misconceptions and biases. When my parents and I began to discuss many of these topics, there were times when we argued, felt hurt, and needed space. But we also knew how important it was for us to be open with one another so we could grow and heal.

Although I intend this workbook to be for parents in the process of adopting, or for those who have recently adopted, any adoptive parent or foster parent who wants to reflect on their choices as well as learn can use it. Many of the activities are great to work on alone, with a partner, or with an agency that offers them as part of their education classes.

My goal for this workbook is to help adoptive parents become more self-aware, to enable them to be supportive of the nuances in adoption, and to help them learn how they can use their power in the adoption community to push for more ethical adoptions and for more supports for adoptees, foster youth, and birth parents. My intention is not to make adoptive and potential adoptive parents feel bad. Instead, I hope to help you work through difficult conversations, encourage you to embrace the history of adoption, and, hopefully, inspire you and prepare you to come together to become parents who are willing to *do the work*, because I know firsthand how helpful it is to have a parent who is willing to listen, learn, and validate our experiences.

I am excited that I was able to collaborate on this workbook with Marcella Moslow, who is a licensed clinical social worker (LCSW) and registered child therapist (RPT). We immediately connected over both of our adoptions from FANA (Foundation for the Assistance of Abandoned Children), an orphanage in Bogotá, Colombia, and how we were just a year apart in age. After I learned that she works as a trauma therapist in adoption and foster care, I had to ask if she'd be willing to contribute some of her professional insight to *WWPSKATA: The Workbook*. Throughout this text you will find expert notes from Marcella that will give you additional insight from her perspective as an adoption-competent therapist.

There are two types of notes from Marcella and they will look something like this:

> NOTE When you see a note like this, it indicates that Marcella Moslow, LCSW, RPT, has some additional guidance to offer.

> LEVEL UP When you see a note like this, it indicates that Marcella is suggesting ways you can broaden your experience and dig deeper.

I would like to point out that you may recognize some text that I've pulled from *What White Parents Should Know about Transracial Adoption*. This workbook can be a companion to that book so together, they can help adoptive parents work through topics more extensively. I have meticulously chosen each excerpt to enable those who haven't read the companion book to complete this workbook on its own, but I recommend that readers purchase both to gain a more comprehensive education. You may also want to keep a designated notebook to write in alongside this workbook.

Before we jump in and get started, please answer the following questions and complete the subsequent activities to begin your journey.

> NOTE In order to allow your best parent-self to be present as you move through the exercises in this book, I encourage you to take a moment to ground and center yourself before answering questions/completing activities. Take some deep breaths, use an affirmation, envision your most present and connected parent-self coming forward, get yourself into a relaxing/comfortable space. Allow yourself to check in with your body, and as you come across sections of the book that stir something in you, pause to be curious about those thoughts/emotions/body sensations that arise.

Have you ever felt that adopting transracially was a bad thing? Why or why not?

What do you know of the history of transracial adoption?

Why did you decide to adopt? What research did you do on the adoption process and the adoption industry prior to making that choice?

ACTIVITY:
ADOPTION AS A HOUSE

Draw an old house and label (or list) some things that have needed/will need to be repaired or replaced over time. Your child can also participate and draw their own version.

1. _____

2. _____

3. _____

4. _____

5. _____

Now let's look at adoption as we would an older house that has been in our family for generations. On the outside the house looks nice enough and it gets the job done. We have a roof over our heads to protect us from storms, we have a place to sleep every night, we have a place where we can keep our clothes and personal items, but the house has some structural issues. The roof is really old and needs to be replaced, the HVAC unit needs maintenance, and the house desperately needs a coat of paint. Because it's the family home, a lot of aunts, uncles, and cousins want to come visit, but they aren't willing to help us pay the bills or invest the time and effort to help us clean it up.

What happens if we keep treating the house this way—if we keep putting off repairs, if we don't do the routine maintenance?

How do you think this relates to adoption?

Right now, adoption as a whole is flawed, but mostly functional. We have the foster system that helps put children in safer homes and we have the private adoption industry that matches babies with couples who want children, but international adoption is akin to the roof of our old house—when we look at it from far enough away, it looks just fine, but when we go up into the attic, we see there is a major leak and it needs a major overhaul.

> LEVEL UP After going through this exercise in which you think of adoption as a house, look at it as if it is an organization. What are some aspects of an organization that need to be replaced/reevaluated over time? What happens if you don't address those areas?

WHY A WORKBOOK?

After publishing *What White Parents Should Know about Transracial Adoption*, I began thinking of what else I could do, and a workbook seemed like the best way to help adoptive families. Although I had included a lot of questions and activities in *WWPSKATA* that I loved, I found that I wished it had the space for parents to keep track of their progress and that they could use to look back on how their experiences affected their opinions over time.

Before we begin, here are a few things you need to know about me.

1. I am not anti-adoption; I am pro family preservation.

2. I believe adoption is sometimes the best available choice.

3. I feel adopted people are the experts in adoption because we have firsthand experience on its impact, but as a community, we need to work *together* to improve the health and well-being of all foster and adoptive children.

4. This workbook is a tool I created to help adoptive parents so they could be better prepared to help adoptees, foster youth, and birth parents.

Although this workbook is aimed at parents relatively new to transracial adoption, you should have general understanding of certain basic vocabulary. If you are unsure and need a refresher, please read *What White Parents Should Know about Transracial Adoption*. You can also add notes as we go along to help you remember various terms.

ACTiViTY:
QUESTiONS ADOPTiVE PARENTS NEED TO ASK THEMSELVES BEFORE ADOPTiNG

To really start things off, I have compiled a few questions that you as potential or current adoptive parents should answer either in the space provided or in a separate notebook so you can look back on it later. In addition, this section includes a short pre-workbook assessment (on page 7). These questions will get you into the right mindset as we reflect on topics covered in *What White Parents Should Know about Transracial Adoption*, and answering them will help us prepare to dive in further and *do the work*.

Take as long as you need to answer the following questions. If you feel yourself getting overwhelmed, feel free to take a break and come back later when you have a clear mind. The purpose of this activity is not to feel like you are taking a test; it is to get an idea of where your (and your partner's) mind is concerning adoption. Please answer the questions as honestly as possible, and do not hold back.

For single parents: Fill out answers in the spaces provided or in a separate notebook so you can look back at them later.

For couples: For best results, fill the questions out separately. Then take some time to discuss both sets of answers in a nonjudgmental environment. Discuss similarities and differences and look back periodically to keep track of your progress.

- What am I hoping to learn? What experiences led me to this workbook and/or *What White Parents Should Know about Transracial Adoption*?

- What kind of anti-racist work am I involved in?

- Are my interactions with people of color sincere?

- How many people of color are in my inner circles? (e.g., family, friends, schools, parenting groups, book groups, gym.)

- Do I have any family members who hold racist beliefs? Y / N

- Do I have racist or prejudiced beliefs? Y / N

- Name an example of current and past biases.

- Am I willing to speak up against prejudiced family members and friends? Y / N

- Do I live in a diverse area? Y / N

- Am I willing to move to a diverse area so my child can have racial mirrors? Y / N

- Why did I choose to adopt a child of a different race/ethnicity than mine?

- Does part of the reason have to do with the extra time I'd have to wait if I only wanted to adopt a white child?

- Why do I think there are more children of color up for adoption?

- What words would I use to describe a birth mother? What do I think they look like?

- Am I comfortable with an open adoption? Why or why not?

- Will I be comfortable explaining my choices to my child one day?

WHO IS THIS WORKBOOK FOR?

This workbook is aimed at potential adoptive/foster parents or current adoptive/foster parents who have adopted cross-culturally. Adoption agencies can also use it as a tool in transracial adoption educational workshops and classes.

HOW CAN THIS WORKBOOK HELP YOU?

WWPSKATA: The Workbook is not a substitution for professional help provided by a therapist, psychiatrist, or physician. If you have any mental health or medical concerns, please consult a physician or *call 911* or the *988* crisis line if you or a loved one has an emergency.

This workbook can help you

- **Learn introductory information:** Future adoptive or foster parents looking to be fully prepared for the complexities of transracial adoption can gain an introduction to transracial adoption by using this workbook.

- **Explore adoptee-centered work:** Families can use this book in conjunction with *WWPSKATA* and other materials to explore the history and impact of transracial adoption.

- **Understand your limitations:** When considering adoption, it is important that you understand your limitations as parents and how your beliefs and the community in which you live can affect the child you adopt.

- **Stay accountable:** In the beginning of the adoption process, it can be easy to take classes, read books, and take part in enriching preparatory activities, but once you become a parent, you can quickly become distracted by doctors' appointments, extracurriculars, and family gatherings and forget to make time for anti-racism work and connecting to your child's culture. This workbook can help prioritize the work with resources, activities, and more.

ACTIVITY:
THE ADOPTIVE PARENT PROMISE

I created an adoptive parent promise based on what I wish my adoptive parents had prioritized when I was first adopted and as my brother and I grew up. I believe you as adoptive and foster parents have a responsibility to the children in your care and that you should create your own promise that will remind you of what is important.

The following is a copy of the adoptive parent promise I wrote for your reference, but after you've reviewed it, please create your own promise. In it, outline the responsibilities you and your family need to prioritize before and after adoption, and sign it before you begin digging into Chapter 1.

As an adoptive parent, I understand that it is my responsibility to learn about and foster ethical adoption practices. I promise to develop and maintain cultural competency so I can teach my children about their race/ethnicity, language, and the traditions of their birth culture. I promise to actively listen to my adopted child and value their opinion as well as the voices of adults who were adopted.

I promise to celebrate my child's race/culture and never let colorblindness cloud my vision. I promise to call out the racism and microaggressions of my friends and family members and protect my child. I promise to believe my child when they tell me they have experienced racism and to support them in any way I can.

I am aware that adoption is multifaceted and that I am coming from a place of privilege that can make it hard to fully empathize with adoptees. Therefore, I promise to do my best by learning more, by asking questions, and by apologizing when I make mistakes. I will support my child no matter how they feel about adoption, and I will engage in an open dialogue, even if I feel defensive. I promise to respect *their* story and only share what my child is comfortable with me telling others online and in person.

Above all, I promise to love my child and never make them feel like they are ungrateful.

signed,

_____

[Adoptive or Foster Parent Signature(s)]

NOTE Ensure that both you and your partner have a say in this promise and that you both agree to uphold it throughout the process of raising your child. When parent/caregiver figures have different parenting approaches, this can lead to added challenges for the child. You may also find it helpful to share this promise with your extended family and others who will be around your child routinely so everyone is on the same page.

ACTIVITY:
WRITE A PERSONALIZED PROMISE AS AN ADOPTIVE PARENT

Choosing to adopt a child of another race can be beautiful and complex. Each family can have a different dynamic, but every parent should remember to prioritize incorporating a child's culture and birth family in their day-to-day lives. After reviewing the material in this workbook, create your own adoptive parent promise that covers how you will put your child's needs first. You can write your promise on the next page, or in a notebook or on a separate piece of paper.

1

ADOPTION BASICS

I n the United States there are a few ways to adopt—internationally, domestically, or privately—and each of these can be either an open or a closed adoption. At a glance, all of these options can seem overwhelming. Unfortunately, this is just the tip of iceberg of what you as adoptive parents need to learn, especially if you are considering transracial adoption. In this chapter, we discuss the basics of adoption, from exploring your desire to adopt, to learning necessary vocabulary, to learning about social media etiquette when you are engaging with the adoption community.

VOCABULARY AND TERMINOLOGY

Let's get started! First, please take some time to look up and write down the definitions for the following terms:

- Domestic adoption

- Private adoption

- International adoption

- Transracial adoption

- Orphan

- Foster parent

- Foster to adopt

- BIPOC

- POC

WHAT IS YOUR WHY?

I decided to become a mom at a very young age. I was twenty-three when I had my first child (biologically), and the experience changed my perspective of families and what love is. Although my decision to have a child was in part influenced by my infertility struggles, I also just felt like part of me wouldn't be complete until I became a mom. From a very young age I loved interacting with children, and when I was old enough to babysit, it was my favorite thing in the world. I felt that being a mom was part of my purpose in life.

Most people have idealistic views of parenthood and how they will choose to parent. As we all know, there are lots of choices—we choose between using formula or breastfeeding, between using cloth diapers or disposable, and we choose whether to allow screen time or highly restrict any screens. Many of us want to believe that we will parent in a certain way, but when we actually have a tiny human to take care of, we quickly learn to adjust our expectations and parenting philosophy.

> NOTE *Child centered* does not mean adoptive parents cannot explore, share, and work through their own feelings and experiences; rather, it means that these feelings and experiences should not overshadow the needs of the child and that making space for the adoptee experience should always be prioritized.

When it comes to transracial adoption, you as parents need to focus on making adoption child centered, but it is also essential that you are honest about your desires and how you first became interested in fostering or adopting a child of color. In the adoptee community there is some controversy about choosing to adopt due to fertility issues and treating it as a backup plan, but when I became a mom, it completely changed my perspective. I knew that parenting was not going to be easy, but I did not understand the weight of becoming a parent physically and emotionally. I didn't understand how deep the desire to parent is—particularly for women and those with a uterus.

We all generally have strong opinions on when and how people should become parents, and it is our responsibility to deal with our baggage and do the work to make sure that we are prioritizing our child's needs before our own. This is why it is important to dig into *your* why so you can engage in a more child-centered approach to adoption.

I've included a list of questions here so you and your partner can reflect on the view you each have of adoption as well as your motivations. Before you move forward in the book, please take the time to answer the following questions. *Please be as honest as possible.*

- When did you decide you wanted to become a parent? How did you envision that occurring? Did you imagine a pregnancy for yourself or a partner? Did you think about adoption when you were younger?

- Please describe what you think a typical pregnancy looks like and the effects of pregnancy on a pregnant person's physical and mental health.

- What type of prenatal care do you think birth parents typically have access to? Do you think that impacts their decision to place their child for adoption?

- What is/was your main motivation for adoption? What is your motivation for adopting a child of another culture?

- Has infertility impacted your decision to adopt? If so, have you consulted with a therapist about the impact infertility has had on your mental health and/or relationship with a partner?

- How has your view of adoption evolved since you adopted?

- Why did you choose this workbook, and how do you think it can help?

- In a perfect world, what would an ideal transracial adoption look like to you (open vs. closed, transracial/international/domestic, etc.)?

- Did you parents discuss race with you as a child? What are your extended family's views on anti-racism?

- What do you most look forward to about adopting transracially?

- How will adopting a child of color impact you and your family?

- What are your extended families' views on adoption? Have you planned to discuss transracial adoption with them?

- Write down your fears or concerns about adoption:

- What support network do you, your partner, and your child have?

- Who are some adoptive parents you look up to? Why?

TOXIC POSITIVITY

> NOTE The toxic positivity mentality is a frequent challenge that I have faced over the years in my clinical work, particularly within adoptive families. Often it is a major reason for the disconnect in the adoptee/adoptive parent relationship. Toxic positivity teaches individuals to deny their own experiences, at least the ones that others deem negative, at the expense of their mental, emotional, and physical health. This leads them to have an overall lack of trust in themselves.

According to *Psychology Today*, *toxic positivity* refers to the idea that staying positive is the only right way to live your life.[1] When I apply this idea to the adoption community, I think it refers to the overarching idea that adoption is always a positive experience and that viewing adoption in this manner is the only proper way to view it. When the dominant narrative in adoption comes from adoptive parents, it is almost a given that this type of toxic positivity will take root and grow. Feel-good stories about adoption are always very popular; it is the more nuanced ones that typically are criticized for diverging from the dominant narrative.

> NOTE A way this type of mentality is also crossing over into schools is with a focus on *growth mindset*. This philosophy can be really helpful for some, but when a child has developmental trauma, they may not be able to access the executive functioning skills they need to apply a growth mindset.

The problem with this toxic positivity is that it lets us forget that race, genetics, and cultural traditions are very important pieces of our families and our personal development. Love is important, but it is beyond essential that adoptive families learn that love also involves learning to accept that adoptees will not always view their adoption in only positive terms.

ADOPTEE CYCLE OF GUILT

If an adoptive child's parents and family do not maintain an objective view of adoption, it can lead to the child bottling up feelings that stray from the happy adoptee narrative. These thoughts can then spiral into a cycle of guilt as they try to understand their feelings about their family versus their feelings about their birth family, and about adoption in general. I refer to this as the *Adoptee Cycle of Guilt*.

NOTE Some of the reasons adoptees keep quiet regarding challenges correlate with the seven core issues of adoption: loss, rejection, shame/guilt, grief, identity, intimacy, and mastery/control.

WE FEEL GUILT: We don't want to make our adoptive parents feel bad and don't want to be seen as ungrateful.

WE FEEL FEAR: We are afraid of rejection, denial, anger, and abandonment. It can be terrifying to open up to our white adoptive parents about racism. We do not want our parents to have any excuse to abandon us when we often already feel like our first families have.

WE FEEL SHAME: We feel shame when we're told we are ungrateful for having negative feelings toward our adoption and that we are selfish for going against the grain of positive adoption language.

WE ARE IN DENIAL: Society often favors a positive narrative of adoption. At times, denying the pain and trauma of being an adoptee can be easier; we can just avoid processing our complicated emotions and experiences.

WE NEED TIME: It can simply take time for us to process and come to terms with our identity problems and experiences as transracial adoptees. And we may not be comfortable sharing that part of our journey with our parents until we are ready.

WE NEED TO BELONG: Being adopted already subjects us to experiences that other people do not have to go through, but speaking about these experiences to our adoptive parents can make them seem more real. It can even be ostracizing to further admit we are different and to point out the issues that we may face that others don't.

NOTE Reasons or root causes for adoptees' lack of disclosure may change based on their developmental stage. It is likely that these underlying issues will all be influential at some point in the adoptee's life, but they can be subtle and hard to detect—all the more reason for you to engage the help of a professional who can assist you in navigating those barriers.

ADOPTEE VOICES

In this section I have included various contributions from transracial adoptees who felt compelled to tell their story. Contributors considered the following questions:

- How has adoption impacted your identity?

- What are some struggles you have had due to adoption?

- How has your relationship with your adoptive parents developed as you explored your identity as an adoptee?

- Did your foster/adoptive parents discuss race?

- Did you feel like you were exposed enough to your birth culture?

- How did your foster/adoptive parents' relationship with race impact your own?

- Did you have an open or closed adoption? How did that impact you?

- What do you wish your adoptive parents would have done?

- If you could tell adoptive parents one thing, what would it be?

- Did you have a relationship with racial mirrors or other transracial adoptees? How did that impact you?

- Did you feel like the system prepared your parents to foster or adopt transracially?

A common critique that my work and previous book, *WWPSKATA*, often gets is that I do not include positive stories of adoption, the ones I do include seem very angry, and it seems as if I curated them to fit my narrative. Although I understand these concerns, I have to point out that there is no shortage of media and articles out there that shine light on happy adoption narratives, so that area has been thoroughly covered. Nevertheless, I've donated some space here for happy stories.

If you feel like it's necessary, include a few positive stories here that you feel are important to spotlight:

If you do have stories that you'd like to include, please use the following space to take the time to elaborate on your need to include happy narratives of adoption when others are sharing the complexities.

Adoptees have a range of experiences with adoption in general and with their adoptive families in particular. Some adoptive children and parents have a fantastic relationship, some are enthusiastic about adoption and are very happy with their experience, and others have the complete opposite experience. All adoptees have a right to share their stories, but on my platform, I am trying to bring awareness to those of us whose voices tend to be silenced.

I ask that you consider this as you read your way through the following pieces. Ask yourself:

- Why do I think this person felt the need to share this piece publicly?

- What can I learn from their experience?

- If this were my child, how could I support them?

- Do I worry about their adoptive parents as I read their work?

And finally, I asked each adopted person to self-identify the way they felt comfortable. What did you notice about how they chose to share their identity?

ANONYMOUS

Birthplace: Vietnam
Age of Adoption: six months old
Country: Canada

"WE ARE THE OUTSIDERS"

My name is [redacted], and I am a twenty-six-year-old Vietnamese Canadian transracial adoptee. My adoptive family consists of my four sisters, one brother, and my two parents. [It is] probably important to mention that one of my sisters was also adopted from Vietnam at a separate time, and my remaining siblings are all Caucasian.

My parents treated me like one of their own and showered me with love and support in anything I did. But the unfortunate reality is my experience was different than my Caucasian siblings, and I feel my parents not having this realization, or simply ignoring it, ultimately led to hardships.

THE MOTTO WAS EQUALITY AND ASSIMILATION

It was the summer of 2020 and I had just begun my work semester with a local engineering firm. As I met each coworker, one after another, there was one introduction that unfortunately stood out. His name was Sam, and the conversion went like this:

"Hello, nice to meet you! My name is Sam, and I am from Europe."

"Hi Sam. I am the new student [redacted], and I am from Newfoundland."

Sam gave me a look I was all too familiar with. He did not believe my answer because of my race.

"But you are not actually from here?! You can't be from here."

These interactions destroy me, so often I opt to give the answer wanted.

"I was born in Vietnam."

"Oh, awesome; we are the outsiders!"

Once he left, I think I was sitting there for hours trying to pick myself back up. Introductions are always stressful for me, but his blatant refusal to see me as a Newfoundlander left me in pieces.

I was in such disarray that I reached out for support from my mother. After thoroughly explaining the situation to her, these were some of her unhelpful words of advice:

- "Oh, [redacted], you can't sweat the little things."

- "You're just going to have to learn to live with it."

- "You are not going to change it."

- "You are never going to be fully accepted."

- "I am not fully accepted here; we learned to live with it."

Growing up, I always had struggles with being a transracial adoptee, but only now, at the age of twenty-six years old can I see it. My mother has always lived in a world of colorblindness, and this was apparent when she dismissed any struggles related to race.

On this day my mother proved to me that her support was conditional.

On this day my mother confirmed to me she is not an ally.

If I could tell my APs [adoptive parents] one thing, it would be that I will always love them, but continuing to ignore my experiences as a POC will only further the distance between us.

LAKE CALDER

Adoptee, foster baby, county court/closed adoption, 1978

"You're a good Italian!"

My adoptive father would proclaim this and wink at me when anyone commented on my features. He reflexively drew attention to his own ethnicity as if I was biologically related to him. My mom would add,

"You have olive skin, like your dad's sister!"

Everyone knew I was adopted, so this made no sense. As a child, I didn't understand what I was seeing in the mirror. Since my parents told me I was Italian, I compared my features to Italian relatives and friends. I grew up thinking I was a mutant Italian girl. I most closely resembled a boy at school. My parents knew he was a biracial adoptee too, but they only befriended the parents of the adopted blonde, blue-eyed girl who could pass as her AP's biological daughter.

In sixth grade, a boy called me the N word on the playground. When I told my parents, they confessed I wasn't Italian, [that] my birthfather's family was Black. My mom said this in a hesitant, whispered tone, as if they were telling me I had a chronic illness, and [they] were afraid someone outside would hear. My adoption was closed and my birthfather was searching for me but had no legal right to contact me. Unlike my birthmother, he wanted to participate in my upbringing and could've connected me to our roots. But he, his three sons, and his huge extended family were denied the opportunity.

I'm privileged that I've only had racial slurs used against me a few times, but the most hurtful one was uttered by my adoptive mother. When I was seventeen and desperate for an identity other than the confused chameleon I'd always been, I dared to wear my hair in braids. When I walked into the kitchen, she made a sour face and muttered,

"I don't like that you look like a *pickaninny*."

I had never heard the word, but I guessed the context had something to do with Black American slaves. If you look up the term, you'll find it referred to as a "racial slur," "archaic," and "derogatory." How could she say that to me? It's beyond insensitive; it's hostile. When I dated non-white guys, she'd say,

"You can be friends with him but you don't want to marry him because . . . life's hard enough . . ."

That was the extent of their racism talk. My godparents were an interracial Chinese/Scandinavian couple and my parents could have said, "Stand up for the person you love and fight ignorance and discrimination." But their takeaway from my godparents' relationship was, "Cower from, and perpetuate racism." My mom failed to consider that the mother of a white boy who brought me home might discourage him from dating me for the same reason. If my non-white boyfriends weren't good enough for her, how could I be good enough for her?

For me, the most hurtful act of racism was my parents' denial of my ethnicity. There is no way to interpret their attempt to pass me as white other than that they felt that my birthfather's heritage was inferior. It was unworthy of acknowledgement, and problematic enough to be concealed. I haven't recovered from the sense of inferiority this instilled in me. I will always feel like I can't meet anyone's standards visually or socially because of my ethnically ambiguous features. As my birthfather says,

"Too white to be Black, too Black to be white."

I'm not what my APs wanted, and that feeling follows me into all relationships, so I never trust that people truly accept me.

I wish my parents had made an attempt to connect my ethnicity with Black history and contributions to global culture.

During the hours of family sitcoms we watched together featuring Black and mixed-race actors I admired, I wish they had said, "You should be proud to have features like these beautiful actresses."

I wish they had examined their own prejudices and waited for a child that represented their ethnic and physical ideal, which was clearly white/European. The adoption system did not prepare them and did not thoroughly vet them as racially sensitive enough for transracial adoption.

Most of all, I wish they had not adopted a child they felt was fundamentally inferior.

Please do not adopt a child without having a network of compassionate people who are happy to provide ethnic mirrors and empowering exposure to the child's ethnicity and culture.

Please never mislead a child about their ethnicity. The effect is devastating to self-worth and self-image. It negatively impacts their ability to trust the adoptive family and potential loved ones in their future.

LESLIE FOLINO

When I was a baby, I was abandoned on the side of the road in southern China. I don't know the whole story, but I was taken to the Guiping Social Welfare Institute in Guangxi where I was adopted by a white couple from Pennsylvania.

At the beginning, my family made an effort to go to Lunar New Year celebrations and Chinese adoptee reunions where I got to play with the Chinese girls who were adopted at the same time I was. Eventually as we grew older and families got busier, we stopped holding reunions, and I haven't talked to those girls in years. With that came the gradual separation between me and my Chinese heritage.

As a kid, I never really cared to learn more about China, its customs, or its language. I was worried about toys and friends and fitting in. My hometown was an affluent, white neighborhood, and that's what I grew used to. I'll be honest, I forgot I was Asian sometimes. Looking back now, I feel like I wasn't raised like I was Chinese in a white neighborhood; I was raised as if I was white. We never really talked about race other than when my parents said they forgot I was Chinese most of the time; they saw me as just Leslie. I love my parents, and I knew they raised me as best as they could, but I wish they taught me about my Chinese culture.

When I reflect on my identity as an Asian American, I feel as if I'm too white to be Asian and too Asian to be white. I look Asian, but I have had the life and experiences of a white person. I get racist comments from white people, and I get invalidated as a Chinese person from Asian people.

When I think about my "otherness," I think about the one time my aunt made a joke replicating a scene from The Christmas Story in which white people go to a Chinese restaurant, and the Asian American servers sing a rendition of "Deck the Halls" in which the refrain is pronounced as "Fa ra ra ra ra" in a heavy accent. My mom initially laughed but told my aunt off for making the joke, but I was kind of taken aback nonetheless. It's times like these where I feel that my family might recognize me as Asian, but only as a "different" Asian. I don't talk in a funny accent or eat funny food, and I grew up in the family, so therefore, I am not the same kind of Asian as those other Asians.

Overall, I don't care that I was adopted, and I'm relatively happy with my upbringing, but I don't know if my parents were taught that they had a duty and responsibility when they adopted from China. Whether they like it or not, I am Chinese, and I am different from them, and that fact shouldn't be ignored. It should be embraced and celebrated and talked about. I think they wanted to ignore the fact that the world would perceive me differently, and I don't blame them.

But no matter how hard that may be as a parent, it's much harder on a kid who doesn't expect how being different can impact them.

ANICA FALCONE-JUENGERT

Anica is a queer, transracial Chinese international adoptee who grew up in the Bay Area, California. They paused earning their bachelor's degree in sociology and are currently working as a human resources assistant and job placement coordinator in the Los Angeles area.

ADDRESS US

Who do we address first?

They gave us our names.
They gave us our culture.
They gave us our homes.

We strive to model after their example.
We strive to become the people who took us from our own.

Who do we address first?

INCURABLE SUPREMACY

I miss what I thought we were,

but I realized your whiteness was not something I could cure. The hours of
    sleep I get are very few.

I wish to no longer be curious about you.

MOVE OUT

B L O C K E D at the door frame.
How dare I walk away—for shame!
I am just like her, just like my other [adoptive] mother. I am at fault for the way
    in which I used a buffer.

Don't pick up the calls, 5 missed rings, I saw—
Keep walking, don't look back. Do not engage in the final attack.

Get in the car. Hit the gas and drive far.

I wish to never return to this house.
This may be the last time I hear her shouts . . .

Am I free?

We will have to wait and see.

FIX [H] ER

Fixer.
I can only coach so much to lift her
spirit that seems to lack a confidence I found in myself that made me
    self-assured.

Fixer.
How can I respond, as a child,
  with our shared experiences that hit her?

What about me?
How come it took me
2 decades to see?

Fixer?
Too bad I couldn't fix her.

LANCE NARKUNAS

MIXED MESSAGES: MEMOIR OF A TRANSRACIAL ADOPTEE

Somewhere in upstate New York . . .

Spring is in full bloom across the deciduous landscape. An overcast sky washes out the late afternoon in a silvery haze. When I am born, they take me from her to be weighed. This is the lightest that I will ever be.

The negotiations were made months prior to my arrival. After a series of meetings behind closed doors, identities are concealed behind a thick line of permanent black ink. I have already been spoken for, and three days later, I go home with strangers. It's Mother's Day.

I've been asked over the years about what it was like when my parents delivered the two words of Earth-shattering reality: *You're adopted.*

This was not my experience. For a secret to be revealed, it must first be kept.

Whenever I would ask my father for the story, his eyes would well with tears.

"They were so young," he would tell me, "but they were smart. She made the right choice, and they loved you very much."

Rather than perpetuate the narrative that I had been saved from the unstable circumstances of an unsustainable upbringing, he always considered himself the lucky one.

His wife felt differently. When my father would share this tale of blessings, of all things, she would correct his grammar tense.

"Say *was* adopted, not *is.*"

It was always clear which side of Nature vs. Nurture she favored, but one is not meant to contend against the other. She lacked my father's understanding that, in order to flourish, nature must be nurtured. Then again, she also lacked his degree in horticulture.

Around the time I began school, I noticed how the features of my peers resembled those of their parents. There are discussions regarding whether an adoptive parent can truly love a child they cannot see themselves in, yet nowhere have I found concern for the child that cannot see themselves in their parents.

I also didn't understand what it meant to be of mixed heritage and race, which were revealed to me in increments. My dark hair and olive complexion came from South Korea (along with my innate dexterity when using chopsticks) while my light eyes and long legs came from Lithuania. Years later in a debate about whether pineapple belongs on pizza, my dad casually mentioned that my birthfather is also of Hawaiian culture, followed with, "You didn't know that?"

There were plenty of things I didn't know. It was like running my tongue over a row of teeth and finding a gap. All I could do was wait for the tooth to grow in.

I recall being assigned a "Family Tree" project in the second grade. My father assured me that the teacher wouldn't take points off for its biological inaccuracy. With his help, I learned how to spell my last name.

He grew up with the communal perspective of an Irish-Italian family, where cousins and relatives were always around when you needed them. For many years he was a genealogy hobbyist, tracing back his family lineage as far back as written records allowed.

While I was welcomed into the culture of my adoptive family, there was no effort or encouragement for me to explore my own roots. Most adoptees I knew were from China or Vietnam. Though their adoptive parents resembled nothing more than white couples on vacation, there were photos of their travels and cultural art preserved to help their children stay grounded in their own identities.

I knew that I was loved, but I wanted to be understood.

A few months after I turned thirteen, I received a package from my birthfather. This was the first time I had any contact with him, though I learned later that my parents had been sending him and my birthmother some updated photos while I was growing up as part of the adoption contract. This is also the first time I was given the letters they both had written for me before the adoption was finalized.

Within this package was a treasure trove of memories he wanted me to have, including a small collection of photos with people who looked like me, a Māori necklace with a hook made of bone, and a book that featured photography and stories of *hapa*, a term reclaimed to represent people of mixed race that are Asian, white, and from the Pacific Islands.

My life is no longer the puzzle of missing pieces that I thought it was, but rather a grand adventure with more to be discovered with every step forward.

I'm told that my first word was *dog*. Ours was a mutt, just like me.

ACTIVITY:
REFLECTION

After reading the essays and poems so thoughtfully created by transracial adoptees, please take a moment to reflect on their stories. A lot of the topics and themes that are common in cross-cultural adoptions focus on identity, love, trauma, and connection. After going through the following questions, think about a moment in your life when you felt misunderstood by your parents or guardians, and ask yourself these questions:

- What do you wish your parents/guardians had done to support you in that moment?

- Did you have a support network?

- How often did you and your friends complain about your parents/guardians?

- Why do you think it is more socially acceptable for non-adopted people to complain and go to therapy, due to their parents' divorce, for example?

LEVEL UP Go through the passages and highlight words/phrases/lines where you noticed a particular emotion or body sensation come up for you (i.e., sadness, anger, defensiveness, a pit in your stomach, tears in your eyes, heart rate increasing). Sit with those emotions and sensations and write about why you think those affected you.

TERMINOLOGY

As you may have noticed after reading the preceding contributions, each adopted person prefers to use different language to describe their adoption and race. I'd like to explore this more and spotlight Marietta Spencer. Spencer introduced the adoption community to a set of adoption language that uses primarily positive terminology.[2] She advocated for leaving behind words like *abandoned* and *real parents* in favor of terms like *placed* and *birth mother*. Spencer thought that using positive language would empower people in the adoption and foster care community while also fighting stereotypes of adoption. This language is often referred to as *positive adoption language (PAL)* or *respectful adoption language (RAL)*.

COMMON LANGUAGE/TERMS

- Gotcha day

- Forever family

- Placed for adoption

- Adoption triad

- Birth mom

- Orphan

- Relinquished

- Better life

- *Adopted* children (as a qualifier used in death announcements, rather than just referring to the kids as children)

- Lost to adoption

- Adoption plan

- Rehoming

- Adoption disruption

- Sibling contact

- Family of origin

- Natural parent

PHRASES ADOPTIVE PARENTS HAVE USED:

- Called to adopt

- God spoke to us.

- Born in my heart

- "She *loved* you so much; she gave you away."

- We were called to adopt.

- We don't see color.

- Tummy mommy

- Referring to adoptees as being "rescued," "saved," "lucky," "ungrateful," "chosen," "bitter," or "angry"

- Referring to birth parents as "your real mom/dad"

- Saying things like "Your story is inspiring."

- Claiming women with an unwanted pregnancy should "just give the child up for adoption."

> NOTE Don't be surprised if as your child ages they want to experiment with different terminology or go back and forth with different wording. Language has a great deal of power, and although we want to ensure trauma-informed language is used, each adoptee is different and will have their own feelings about terms. The most important thing is that they choose (and are supported with) wording that they feel accurately reflects their experience.

Adoptive parents often advocate for people to use PAL, and I urge you to question *why* adoptive parents and prospective adoptive parents feel more comfortable using it. Why are they more comfortable framing their narrative with phrases that often sugarcoat what many adoptees feel happened? Often as an adoptee, I feel abandoned, given up. My thoughts toward my adoption are complicated at best, and every time I see an adoptive parent "correct" an adoptee online for using more realistic language, it is frustrating.

As adoptees, we need support and honest language when it comes to discussing adoption experiences. We will never have perfect terminology that doesn't offend anyone, but there are better options depending on who you are talking to in the community. Adoptive parents and even birth parents will have language that they prefer because it makes them feel better, but adoptees tend to prefer language that suits the nuanced emotions adoption triggers in them. And the truth is that there is no one-size-fits-all language. But what many adoptees agree on is that we do not appreciate or care for PAL. We find it offensive.

One parent I spoke with anonymously shared the following learning experience.

In the first few weeks, my legacy language was still there. I'd refer to my biological kids as my kids and imply my third child wasn't mine. I felt terrible. My middle child did the same sort of thing, saying "don't hurt my brother," but now she would say, "don't hurt your big brother," that sort of thing.[3]

Remember that you will make mistakes along the road. It happens. What is important is that you are able to acknowledge your missteps and learn from those experiences. Make sure you are validating your child's feelings and respecting their preferences as to what type of language they prefer. Do not fall back on excuses and nicknames that you personally prefer because you find them cute. Do not use terms such as *Coconut* or describe your child's skin color using foods because these can often be perceived as microaggressions.

You will find some terms more favorable; just remember, an adoptee should be able to reserve the right to correct you at any point and ask you to refrain from using certain language in conversations. Certain words and phrases can be very triggering to hear, so it is important to support adoptees instead of arguing with them and rejecting their opinion because you don't agree with it. Of the almost one hundred different comments by adoptees who answered a quick poll on Twitter, most seemed to show similar distaste for PAL.[4] To get you started, here are a few of the terms and phrases I personally use.

ONEST ADOPTION LANGUAGE

- Refer to birth parents as First Mom, First Dad, or simple "Mother" or "Father."

- Do not say it was "God's plan" or things to that effect.

- Engage in honest discussions of the adoptee's adoption story that are age appropriate.

- Don't refer to a child being adopted as being "surrendered for adoption" or similar language.

Of course, every family is different, so it is important to check in with your foster children or adoptive children periodically to make sure the language the family is using is still appropriate. Adoptees may feel differently from year to year, and giving them the autonomy to decide what language their family and friends use to refer to adoption can be very empowering for them. Start by going through the list of common adoption language and add new terms as you learn them. Once you have a comprehensive list, ask yourself the following questions and document your answers in the spaces provided:

- Why do words or phrases you've read or heard before make you uncomfortable?

- Are there any other words that you do not prefer? Why?

- If you have a child, which words does the adopted child or foster youth prefer?

- Which words does the child wish to be off limits?

- How can you advocate for your current or future child?

- Ask yourself, "Which language is my go-to language?"

LEVEL UP Where did you first hear this type of language? Was this the language you were brought up using? If so, why do you think that was?

SUPPLY AND DEMAND

From my experience reading through adoption groups, I noticed that many adoptive parents prioritize the following aspects of the adoption process:

1. The speed of the process

2. The cost, including fees for home study, lawyers, travel, and so on

3. Whether to foster or adopt domestically or internationally

Historically, adoptions in the United States have been based on "matching" children to adoptive parents to uphold racially homogenous families.[5] State laws that govern part of adoption processes and are not monitored by any federal agency allow a free-market dynamic that focuses on supply and demand.[6] Reports of primarily Black or mixed-race children being adopted *from* the United States to Canada, England, Spain, Italy, and France started appearing in 2004.[7] But if over a million couples are looking to adopt in the United States, why are children being adopted into other countries? Because the majority of prospective white adoptive parents, who make up 70 percent of adopters, prefer to adopt white children.

> NOTE I highly recommend that the families I work with read *Adoption: What You Should Know*, by Janine Myung Ja to learn more about the history of adoption throughout the world.

There is a racial hierarchy defined as *colorism* where lighter skin is preferred over darker.[8] Colorism is alive and well in the adoption process and industry. Agencies have been shown to charge adoptive parents a higher fee to adopt a white infant than to adopt a Black infant. The majority of adoptions of white infants occur domestically and can range from $4,000 to $30,000, whereas the adoption costs of Black children, who are primarily adopted from foster care, range from $0 to $2,500. When you look at children considered "closer to white" that are available through international adoption from preferred countries like China, Russia, Guatemala, Korea, and Romania, the costs range from $7,000 to $25,000—further evidence of colorism.[9]

> NOTE Colorism is an issue across the globe, and children become aware of it quite young. Research shows that even young Black children demonstrate some bias in favor of whiteness. Whiteness is connected with being pretty, smart, or good, whereas blackness is associated with being dumb, ugly, or bad.

Children can be lumped into categories that best fit the adoption industry. Some even categorize children based on their proximity to whiteness and whether they can be considered honorary white due to a history of assimilation in America. Some of the countries that are often considered honorary white in international adoption agencies include China, Korea, India, Taiwan, Japan, Thailand, and Mexico.[10] Another category listed in agency reports/options includes darker-skinned Latinos and Southeast Asians, often referred to collectively as Black. Some of the countries in this category include Cambodia, the Philippines, Vietnam, Haiti, Ethiopia, Nigeria, and Liberia.[11]

Agencies know that there is often a demand for white babies and children. Due to that demand, they label children according to their proximity to whiteness based on adoptive parents' trends and preferences. So, although adoptive parents may be open to adopting a child of color, many show preferences for adopting mixed-race children or other children of color who are closer to passing as white. When agencies cater to this desire and set up their categories, it's not just a coincidence that they can charge more adoption fees for such preferences.

The *theory of cognitive dissonance* refers to the psychological discomfort that individuals feel when faced with conflicting beliefs, behaviors, or attitudes. When applied to the adoption industry and the way adoptive parents react when faced with the nuances and sometimes ethical issues of the process, we can see how the need to reduce dissonance can pressure them to avoid certain hard truths like the trauma in adoption.[12]

Some ways people work to ease the discomfort of cognitive dissonance are the following:

1. They change their behavior to bring it more in line with the opposing belief.

2. They justify the behavior by changing one of their beliefs.

3. They develop new beliefs to help justify their behavior.[13]

And when you look at the dominant belief in the adoption industry, that "love makes a family and color doesn't matter," you can see the need to justify why agencies and adoptive parents make their preferences of an adopted child's race/ethnicity known.

How can we believe the voices of our adoptive families when they tell us they don't see color when so much evidence shows us that race does matter? Race factors into the decisions adoptive parents make from the moment they fill out the adoption paperwork. From the moment a parent chooses adoption, they have the choice to choose race . . . because it does matter to adoptive families—so much so that US-born Black and mixed-race babies are being adopted to countries like Canada, where birth parents in the United States may think racism is less of an issue due to agencies that are starting to require courses to heighten racial sensitivity.[14]

Why do agencies ask potential adoptive parents about their preferences? Why do more white couples prefer mixed-race children? The adoption community justifies these preferences to reduce the discomfort they and adoptive parents feel of their belief that race doesn't matter. The evidence showing that a child's race and ethnicity is important to adoptive parents makes it apparent that color does matter. And transracial adoptees see that. We see our differences, how our family ignores our race when it makes them more comfortable, and how they embrace our differences when it supports their narrative that love is the answer.

ACTIVITY:
FLIP THE SCRIPT

With many agencies, potential adoptive parents are often expected and/or required to fill out forms that describe the children they are comfortable adopting into their family. They are expected to list qualifiers like these:

- What race is your preference or which races would you be willing to adopt?

- What age range are you most interested in/comfortable with adopting?

- Do you require/prefer an open or closed adoption?

- Are you willing to adopt a child where there's a history of drug use in utero?

- What range of disability are you comfortable considering when adopting?

- And much more

For this activity, I would like you to flip the script and put yourself in the shoes of the adopted child. Write out qualifications you think they would have for an adoptive family. Please be as specific as possible and consider some of the questions your family has been asked about what you are open to.

ADOPTED CHILD PREFERENCES:

- What age do you prefer the adoptive parents to be?

- What race of parents are you open to and why?

- Are the parents willing to adopt sibling groups? Up to how many?

- Are they supportive of open adoption? How so?

- What health statuses are the parents comfortable with?

  - What disabilities are they open to?

  - Are they open to adopting a child with a mental illness diagnosis?

- What are their religious beliefs?

- Political beliefs?

- What is their marriage status?

- Do they have a history of abuse?

- Do they have any biological children? If so, how many?

  - 0

  - 1–2

  - 3–4

  - 5+

- Do they have any adopted children? If so, how many?

  - 0

  - 1–2

  - 3–4

  - 5+

- Are they open to adopting a child who has a history of therapy?

- What is the makeup of the community in which the prospective parents live (i.e., diversity statics)?

- Do the parents work on anti-racism?

  - No

  - Beginner

  - Very involved

  - Expert

- Are the people who surround and support the parents anti-racist (i.e., coworkers/friends/family)?

- What is their parenting strategy?

- How do they feel about work/life balance?

- Are they good with finances?

- How would you prefer parents to handle racism from strangers/friends/family?

Write your own ideas for questions/qualifications here:

I posed questions like these in a condensed format on my Instagram page (@adoptee_thoughts) and shared my preferences to start: Open to Latino parents or parents who embrace my heritage and will teach me Spanish. Need to live in a diverse community and support an open adoption. Not open to Republicans or pro-lifers.

Here were some other adoptees preferences.[15]

- Domestic adoption that would stay local to where birth family is located

- Not adopting for infertility reasons

- Open to child of any gender; not seeking out male or female specifically

- Parents who have dedicated time and energy to healing from their past trauma

- No conservatives

- Not adopting because of saviorism

- Parents must be BIPOC

- Seeking parents dedicated to encouraging an open adoption and contact with birth family

LEVEL UP Reflect on your response to reading those preferences. Were there parts of you that felt rejected? Defensive? Hurt? Do you feel that if the child you adopted held any of these preferences that it would impede your ability to parent/connect with that child?

ACTIVITY:
GET UNCOMFORTABLE BEING UNCOMFORTABLE

Write down a moment in which you felt alone in a room full of people—friends, family, strangers at the supermarket. Share how you felt isolated and alone and think about the following:

- Did you look different than everyone around?

- Did you have an accent?

- Or were you the only one who didn't speak the language?

Here's an example:

You are a single dad who was in a parenting class where 99 percent of the participants were mothers.

- Yes, I looked different. Everyone but me was female and I stood out.

- My voice was deeper so every time I spoke, my voice would automatically draw everyone's attention.

- We all spoke English . . . but it was like I wasn't in on the lingo, the inside jokes, etc.

Now write down a situation in which your future child or current child who was adopted transracially might have experienced that same isolation. If you are having difficulty coming up with such a situation, you can fill in the blanks in the following example or share in the blank box provided.

_____ was _____ years old, and in her _____ (class, sports meetup, camp, family gathering, etc.) she was (number) _____ of (how many)_____ children who were (adopted, BIPOC, etc.) _____.

Now that you have shared your child's potential or actual experience, I would like you to think about ways you can support children that may make you nervous or uncomfortable.

Here are some ideas.

- Taking a foreign language class or a Black history class

- Going to Latino, Asian, or Black community parades

- Eating at authentic BIPOC restaurants

- Moving to a diverse neighborhood

Please share some activities you have done or will do to help learn more about the child's culture.

1.

2.

3.

How can you make these experiences less uncomfortable?

Why is it important to push outside your comfort zone?

What do you learn and experience when you engage in events and with communities that you typically are not exposed to?

How does it benefit your child? Or how will it if you have not adopted yet?

Have you ever been in a situation in which you were the only (or one of a few) person of your race/ethnicity in a room? How did it make you feel?

TRANSRACIAL AND INTERNATIONAL ADOPTION

Intercountry adoption was uncommon until after World War II, when children who were orphaned were sent to the United States from Germany, Japan, and Greece. The Korean and Vietnam wars promoted an even larger surge of intercountry adoptions, often involving mixed-raced children. Before this, many countries did not have laws to protect the best interests of children being adopted abroad.[16]

Arguments against transracial and international adoption focus on forced global migration and the exploitation of poor countries. Since adoption is advantageous for white, middle-class infertile couples, some couples can forget the injustices that face poor women of color and poor white women. One of the first groups to argue against transracial adoption was Black social workers in the 1970s; they believed that transracial adoption threatened the personal development of Black children's identities and thought that white parents would be ill-prepared to help Black children against racism. Their claims are supported by the mixed results of the few studies that have been done on identity and development.[17]

Other arguments focus on ethics, abuse in orphanages, fraud, and kidnapping. Some countries even started believing that intercountry adoption should be avoided and that the solution was to care for children within their birth country instead of adopting children out. Still others argue that international adoption violates human rights because it deprives children of their heritage birthright.[18] In countries like Australia and New Zealand, the transracial adoption of Aboriginal and Māori children is viewed by many as cultural genocide. In Switzerland, the adoption of Roma children is seen as similarly problematic.[19]

Despite the arguments, international adoptions are still very much in play. Often adopting from a poor country of origin is seen as easier than adopting children, especially Black children, from the foster care system.[20] Congress passed the Multiethnic Placement Act (MEPA) in 1994 and removed race from consideration for adoptive placements.[21] This made it easier for white, middle-class adoptive parents to adopt children of other races since the law did not form any federal guidelines; it left it up to adoption agencies to provide racial and cultural education. The problem with this is that the requirements that adoptive parents fulfill (i.e., racial competency, home studies, income, etc.) vary from each agency and state; some states still only require potential adoptive parents to fill out a questionnaire concerning their attitudes toward race, and some require actual classes. Despite how it claims to increase the number of foster and adoptive families, MEPA does not mandate federal or even state funding to increase the outreach efforts to families of color.[22]

MEPA made colorblind placement legally mandatory in the US, except for Native American children who were subject to the Indian Child Welfare Act (ICWA). This federal law that governs the out-of-home placement of Native children passed in 1978 to protect Native American families from a biased welfare system. Prior to passage, Native Americans were three times more likely to be forcibly removed from their families of origin than non-Native children, and they were coerced into abusive boarding schools that stripped them of their customs, culture, and language. Between approximately 1860 and 1978 there were over 350 government-funded, often church-run boarding schools in the US; during this same time frame, the United States broke treaties and policies and started taking more tribal lands.[23]

Despite its implementation concerns, the ICWA has been labeled the gold standard of adoption laws by over eighteen child advocacy organizations.[24] It is important to note that even though ICWA emphasizes how important culture, community, and elders are, the law is not based on race but rather citizenship or membership in a federally recognized tribe. Despite the protection the ICWA afforded, white families have filed challenges over the years in order to adopt Native children, including some that had Native relatives who were seeking custody.[25] So while the ICWA offers some great protections, there are still loopholes, and if we compare the laws and protocols enacted domestically versus internationally, there are some significant differences in each.

ACTIVITY:
IS IT DISCRIMINATION OR IS IT CULTURAL PRESERVATION?

It is important to note that currently ICWA is being brought before the Supreme Court in the case of Brackeen v. Haaland. At the time of this book going to print, three white couples are expected to have their case heard in court. They claim that ICWA discriminated against them because of their race. Please take some time to look up the case, the results, and the impact it has had on Indigenous communities and adoption policies in the United States and answer the following questions.[26]

1. Why do you think some people see ICWA as discrimination? Do you agree or disagree?

2. How does ending ICWA benefit white couples?

3. How does ending ICWA benefit Indigenous children?

4. What are the concerns with losing ICWA?

5. How can adoptive parents support Indigenous children and families?

IS ADOPTION CHILD CENTERED?

The Hague Convention on the Protection of Children and Cooperation in Respect of Intercountry Adoption (shortened to the Hague Adoption Convention) mandates that countries protect the child's best interests. It aims to prevent the sale of, abduction of, or trafficking of children. According to the Hague Adoption Convention, intercountry adoption should be considered as a last option when a child has been deemed eligible for adoption; first, due consideration by the orphanage/agency needs to be given to finding an adoption placement in the child's country of origin.[27] Despite the Hague Adoption Convention's mandate, international adoption is seen as a first option by people wanting to adopt, often because adoptive parents' preferences are met more easily and with shortened wait times.[28]

Because adopting multiracial and biracial children became preferred when white babies weren't available for adoption in the 1950s, adoption agencies began bending the social norms of racial categorization of adoptees, particularly for Black adoptees, to avoid the "one-drop rule" in favor of labeling infants with both Black and white heritage as multiracial. By including "white" or "multiracial" when labeling children up for adoption, adoption agencies have increased the adoptability of children considered as multiracial since research of pre-adoptive decisions has revealed a preference of "part-white" children among white adoptive couples.[29] This means white couples prefer and are more accepting of adopting multiracial and biracial children the closer they are to their perceived idea of whiteness.

> NOTE This is an example of how adoption is not adoptee centric; rather, it prioritizes the adoptive parent's comfort level rather than the needs of the child.

Adoptive parents prefer adopting multiracial children because they believe they will have more in common with them and because they feel more legitimate by sharing racial ties with their adopted children. They also often feel less guilt for taking the children away from their community of origin and that mixed-race children will be less visibly different and "easier to explain" to relatives, friends, and neighbors.[30]

Please consider this information as we look at the data in the following table and the accompanying sidebar.

Table 1. Change in Number of Adoptions by Race and Ethnicity[31]

RACE AND ETHNICITY	ADOPTIONS IN 2005–2007	ADOPTIONS IN 2017–2019	PERCENTAGE CHANGE IN NUMBERS OF ADOPTIONS
White	64,626	91,185	41%
Black	41,471	32,342	–22%
Hispanic	28,400	38,755	36%
Other	10,125	20,329	101%
Total[a]	152,088	185,267	22%

[a] Total includes children with missing or insufficient information on race and ethnicity.

———— AVAILABLE ADOPTION SITUATIONS[32] ————

African American baby due any day. $17k + legals

Biracial (AA/NA) girl due August 18. $22.5k + $2.k legals + medical

Biracial (CC/HISP) baby due September 15. $30.5k + $4.5k legals

African American girl due September 26. $17k + $6–8k medical

Biracial (CC/AA) girl due October 12. $25k +$8–10k medical

African American girl due October 15. $17k +4.5k legals

African American boy due October 22. $17k + $6–8k medical (Mom smokes cigarettes)

Biracial boy due late October. $30k +$7k legals

Caucasian baby due late October. $28K + $8k legals

African American baby due November 18. $17k +6–8k medical (Mom smokes cigarettes)

Caucasian baby due in February. $29k +$7k legals (Mom would like an open adoption with a few visits per year)

When we look at the two sources of information provided by the Administration for Children and Families, a division of the US Department of Health and Human Services, we can see some interesting statistics about adoption in the United States.

Table 1 shows that the number of adoptions of Black children has decreased significantly between 2017 and 2019, but the number of children in the Other category has more than *doubled*. The Other category mostly consists of children who are considered multiracial. We can take an educated guess as to why this category has doubled and there is a sudden uptick in multiracial children being adopted compared to the trends from the earlier years.

In the US, laws like MEPA are meant to protect children and families for considering race in placement, but the unfortunate reality is that race, despite it being a social construct, often has real ramifications in how people, even children, are treated. As mentioned earlier, agencies can charge different fees depending on the race of the children who being adopted. And although the Available Adoption Situations sidebar does not have a multiracial designation, we can see that the fees for biracial children are *higher* than they are for Black children.

> Why do you think that is? When you consider this harsh reality, how do you think it makes BIPOC expectant parents feel?

ADOPTING CHILDREN FROM THE UNITED STATES

Did you know that some expectant parents are so worried about the racial injustices in the US that they choose to place their children in families outside of the United States?

Despite the categorization that goes on, birth mothers of Black, Brown, and mixed-race babies often think that their children would have better lives outside of the racialized climate here in America. This is why babies are still being adopted to countries like Italy, Canada, the Netherlands, and Germany. Susan, a white American mother who adopted a multiracial child, said in an interview for CNN that "there's too much prejudice over here. The white people are going to hate him because he is half Black, and the majority of Black people are going to hate on him because he's half white."[33]

Many birth parents who choose to place children via international adoption out of the United States believe that they will not experience as much discrimination in other countries like the Netherlands. Others have personal experiences within the foster care system that make them fear similar abuses for their children if they are left in the system, and so they also choose a couple not in the US. In 2010, the US State Department counted only forty-three children who were adopted overseas, but the Netherlands, Germany, and Switzerland combined reported around 205 children who were adopted from the United States.[34]

Adoptive families often say that they want to give a child a safe and loving home; they often emphasize their pure intentions. . . but at the end of the day, the adoption industry is a business. That said, although agencies put price tags on babies and children, adoptive parents have the power to put pressure on the industry to have more ethical practices.

How can adoptive parents address race-based pricing in adoption?

1. Reach out to adoption agencies and hold them accountable by asking questions and filing complaints about raced-based pricing.

2. Refuse to work with agencies that continue to use raced-based fees.

3. Create a petition to stop race-based pricing in the agencies near you.

4. Raise awareness in your local community by talking openly about this issue on social media, with news contacts, or even in letters to local leaders.

NOTE Adoptive parents have a responsibility to promote and advocate for changes in ethical practices surrounding adoptions. Taking on this responsibility (when done appropriately) is a way to strengthen your relationship with your child by acknowledging that the system is flawed.

FOSTER CARE

The foster care system was originally created in the 1930s to provide care for homeless and neglected children during the Great Depression. In the 1980s, it evolved into a social service aimed at healing youth with emotional, psychological, and behavioral issues, typically caused by abuse they experienced. The number of Black and Indigenous children in foster care is double that of their representation in the general child population. Ethnic minorities are more likely to be represented in foster care due to the disparate treatment that minorities face. Black children are more likely than any other ethnic group to be referred to protective services and have allegations of abuse substantiated.[35]

Black children are also less likely to be reunified with their birth families and more likely to experience longer stays in foster care, which has become a large reason why more Black children than white children are awaiting adoption. Compared to other children, studies have discovered that Hispanic children are more likely to remain in out-of-home placements for longer periods, are more likely to receive fewer mental health services, and are also less likely than white children to be adopted out of foster care.[36]

Most prospective adoptive parents tend to be well educated, affluent, white Americans. In certain states, structural barriers prevent more racially diverse prospective parents from adopting, including marriage requirements, policies against couples who are LGBTQ+, and cultural biases by public adoption agencies that are less likely to approve Black applicants. Potential adoptive parents also show a preference for same-race placements, and the 25 to 35 percent of prospective parents who are open to adopting children of a different race show a higher preference for younger children. This is one reason why MEPA received support to help place children who are likely to age out of foster care in adoptive homes since many studies have shown the benefits of placing a child for adoption are significant. When a child is adopted, they are more likely to have a stronger sense of belonging, be more resilient, and have better financial outcomes such as being more highly educated and more financially well-off.[37]

Despite this, some child welfare professionals adamantly argue against placing children of color in foster care with white adoptive parents. This is largely due to a deficit in the ethnic identity development of transracial adoptees in white families. In fact, transracial adoptees experience a more significant drop in ethnic identity levels than children placed with parents of the same race.[38]

It is a pressing concern, in general, that children of color in the child welfare system face more disparities than their white counterparts, are less likely to be reunified with their birth family, are less likely to be matched with a permanent family, and are more likely to be placed in care settings.[39] The National Council on Crime and Delinquency has also found that girls, especially girls of color, in the foster care system have a higher recidivism rate, meaning that they are more likely to reenter the juvenile justice system than girls who have never had contact with the welfare system.[40] So when children of color are less likely to be placed in a permanent home, it can increase their risks when their time in the welfare system is prolonged.

It is essential to sit with the history of the foster care system and the adoption industry before you move forward in the adoption process.

SOCIAL MEDIA ETIQUETTE

Whether you are adopting through foster care or privately, you may find yourself googling and following families on Instagram, TikTok, Facebook, or YouTube. Considering that the adoption process can often be very slow, following creators on socials can help make the process a little less nerve-wracking and, as a bonus, you can find some wonderful friends. Still, it is very important that current and prospective adoptive/foster parents be vigilant about what and how they share information online.

As an adoptee I've seen that some adoptive parents are picking up the habit of using hashtags meant for adoptees (e.g., #adopteevoices) when posting pictures of their child, and honestly this needs to stop ASAP. It is important to remember that pictures of your child, with the caption written by you, is *not* an adoptees voice, and even if your child gave you permission to post, that is still inappropriate until they are at least eighteen. Many adoptees don't share the truth of how they feel about being adopted with their adoptive parents when they are little.

As adoptive parents, you need to think about the power you hold and the harm that it can cause adoptees (aka a marginalized community) if used incorrectly. If you choose to engage on social media, it is your responsibility to remember not to speak for the adoptee experience unless you yourself were adopted, and to think critically about what is and isn't okay to share. I've created a quick activity to help adoptive parents.

ACTiViTY:
DOES iT CROSS THE LiNE?

Please look at the following examples and explore whether or not you think they are appropriate. Think about the gray zones and why operating in them may be harmful to adoptees and birth parents.

GOOGLE ADS

Look up "adoptive parent searching" on Google and write down three examples of profiles or websites that come up. *Do you think any cross a line?*

SOCIAL MEDIA PROFILES

Many hopeful adoptive parents will hear the advice that they should start sharing information about themselves and their families. They might be told this by agencies or past adoptive parents who say that have found such sharing to be helpful in "matching" with a birth parent. Search the hashtag #hopingtoadopt and ask yourself the same question:

Do these profiles cross a line? Is there a way to share responsibly?

Create your own Instagram post. In the space provided on the left, include a picture of your family as is and what you think would be appropriate to share. Now create another post on the right that you think crosses the line.

What are the similarities and differences? If you were an adoptee or birth parent, which parts do you think you'd find hurtful or uncomfortable?

YOUTUBERS ADOPTING PUBLICLY

There are many YouTubers who will share the entire process of searching for and adopting a child. Look up one or two and explore the same question:
Does it cross a line?

NOTE Keep in mind that many agencies also put out ads for children in which such personal information is being shared. Have you ever thought about whether those children/their biological families provided consent for that information to be shared? Have you thought about whether it's even accurate? Why is it that sometimes you may come across similar language for different children? Imagine what it would feel like for that child if they were ever to see that ad. What do you think that would model in terms of healthy boundaries and online safety?

HOW CAN ADOPTIVE PARENTS ENGAGE APPROPRIATELY ONLINE?

Although social media can be a wonderful place to connect with the adoption community, it is important for adoptive and foster parents to remain responsible, respectful, and considerate of adoptees, foster youth, and birth parents that have had complex experiences. Many adoptees and birth parents that I know have recently started to explore the nuances and trauma of adoption and are often expressing themselves freely for the first times in their lives.

I understand that it can be difficult to hear from adoptees who are quickly labeled "angry" and that their words can cause some defensiveness, confusion, and even anger in you, but just because you do not like to read posts or watch videos that make you uncomfortable, it doesn't mean you have the right to speak over adoptees, foster youth, or birth parents. If you are set on absorbing content online and/or engaging with the adoption community, here are a few tips to keep in mind.

1. **Branch out from what makes you comfortable.**

   One common mistake that I see adoptive parents make is surrounding themselves in a bubble online. They follow dozens of adoptive or foster parents online but haven't branched out to learn about and support those in the adoption community that are the most impacted by it. It can be easy to follow an adoptive parent that you admire and comment on their happy pictures and videos on your highly curated Instagram feed, but it can be difficult to follow and learn from profiles that share a less positive perspective.

   Aim to make your feeds reflect a diverse array of experiences and lives. This will help you branch out and learn about different perspectives in our community.

2. **When in doubt, stay silent and move on.**

   Undoubtedly you will come across accounts and creators that make you sad, uncomfortable, or even angry. It's okay to unfollow, block, and move on with your day. Although I do strongly suggest that you get comfortable being uncomfortable, I'd rather you make progress a little at a time than find yourselves burned out and unwilling to engage and do the work. We are all human, and you have every right to feel a certain way. Just remember to be respectful of your own boundaries and needs so you can be there for your child and be willing to grow over time.

> NOTE I often recommend that when joining/following new social media pages that are about adoption, you take at least one month where you do not post/comment but rather commit to listening and reflecting.

3. **Ask for help respectfully, but don't expect it for free.**

Remember that you are responsible for your education and current/future adoptive children. The adoption community does not owe you free consultations and conversations that involve emotional labor. If you are learning from someone on social media, check out their websites and the services they offer, and send them an inquiry via email, their form, or politely in their direct messages.

If cost is an issue, remember that so many free resources are available to the public online or at your local library. Remember that adoptees who share their stories online get dozens of messages every day from current and prospective adoptive parents. Many of us have tried helping so many families in the past (because we want to help adoptees/former foster youth), but we have also been burned by disrespectful individuals who have taken advantage of our time and energy.

CHAPTER 1 REFLECTION QUESTIONS

- How can you help children without benefitting from a corrupt system built on systemic racism?

- Do you feel like fostering and adoption are a type of white saviorism? Why or why not?

- Do you think there are ways to encourage family preservation?

- Do you feel equipped to raise a child of color?

- How do you think a parent of color parents differently than you do as a white person?

- What benefits are there to children of color being raised by other people of color?

- What do you bring to the table that a birth parent can't? That a BIPOC can't?

- Can you explain the seven core issues in adoption?

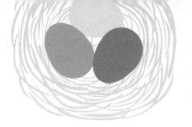

2

ETHICAL, SAFETY, AND TRAFFICKING CONCERNS

A doption, fostering, and guardianship are all systems that are supposed to be child centered—meaning that the needs of the child's mental and physical health as well as their safety are put first—always. Unfortunately, that is not always the case. There has been an unfortunate history of abuse, neglect, and even trafficking within adoption in the United States.

Even though I love my adoptive parents and they loved me and raised me to the best of their abilities, that does not mean that they didn't make mistakes. Their love doesn't negate the harm they caused me. Adoptive parents are human; they aren't infallible. Mistakes happen, but it's when adoptive parents refuse to change, learn, and do better that it's a problem. Not all adoptive parents are amazing and not all are awful. But just as we accept that some are the best damn parents around, we also need to accept that some are horrible and abusive.

NOTE Parents being able to reflect upon and acknowledge mistakes or lack of knowledge regarding certain topics is extremely important to building and strengthening a relationship with children in your care. Many adoptive parents have good intentions; however, good intentions do not outweigh the harmful impacts that the lack of education and/or acknowledgment can have on the adoptee.

And we need to listen to adoptees and make sure that those prospective parents who aren't prepared, who aren't willing to work on themselves and make progress, aren't able to adopt. Maybe then social workers won't be pressured to pass adoptive parents during initial checks.[1] Maybe we'd hear fewer horrible news stories about adopted children who have been abused and/or killed if we actually used and perfected the current system that is supposed to vet adoptive parents. But in order for this to happen, in order for the system to protect adoptees, the adoption industry needs to admit to their mistakes.

They could start by hiring adoptees, hiring birth moms, and creating programs that don't revolve around a for-profit system based on systemic racism. Like I said, I love my parents. They love me. But love isn't enough. It's time to do the work.

Child trafficking is defined as the recruitment, transfer, harboring of, or receipt of a child for the purpose of sexual or labor exploitation or slavery.[2] *Illegal adoptions* are defined as those that result from abduction, sale, or trafficking in children, fraud, falsification of official documents, or coercion.[3] When you think about child trafficking and illegal adoption practices, you might think that they seem like a problem of the past, like the Baby Scoop Era or Operation Babylift, but there are still instances that occur today.

In this chapter we will be discussing the history of abuses and how adoptive parents can look for red flags and help advocate for more regulation and oversight to protect foster and adoptive children.

UN-ADOPTED

Although legal in some states, the practice of rehoming a child is highly unethical. *Rehoming* is when adoptive parents transfer custody of a child to another person or family without involving the child welfare or government agencies.[4] One rehoming case in particular that sticks out for me is that of the infamous family YouTuber Myka Stauffer and her adopted son Huxley. She and her husband created a profitable YouTube channel with over 700,000 fans that took off in 2014 after she shared their journey to adopt Huxley; then she announced that they were placing him in a new home that could better address his medical needs.[5]

When discussing the rehoming of children, it is important to know that, in America, anywhere from 10 to 25 percent of adoptions are disrupted and about 1 to 5 percent are dissolved. *Disruptions* refer to when an adoption is ended and the child is returned to foster care or new adoptive parents before the original adoption becomes legally finalized. *Dissolutions* or *dissolved adoptions* occur after a finalized adoption—when the child's relationship with their adoptive family is legally severed and the child is then placed in foster care or with new adoptive parents.[6]

Why do you think disruptions/dissolutions occur?

What type of services do you think are necessary to help prevent the rehoming of children?

Although Second Chance Adoptions' (a division of Wasatch International Adoption Agency) practice of placing children in state-approved homes is not technically considered rehoming because it involves welfare agencies, the agency and process are (supposedly) more ethical. In an interview with *The Atlantic*, Executive Director Kathy Kaiser stated that posting photographs and personal details of the children is meant to "show the human" side of them. It is also important to note that very limited statistics are available on these types of adoptions due to a lack of oversight and paperwork. For instance, birth certificates and social security cards are often changed, but a good number of the children are children of color or were adopted internationally at some point.[7]

NOTE Rehoming is an extremely dehumanizing practice and can have lasting adverse effects on children. Children who are rehomed may have low self-esteem, feel chronic shame, or believe they are damaged and have difficulty building healthy attachments. Impacts can also include reduced trust that their needs will be met or that appropriate attunement will be provided, avoidance of intimacy/closeness with others, and feelings of being a burden to others. Rehoming is a dangerous practice and demonstrates a lack of regard for the mental, emotional, and physical health and safety of the children.

ACTIVITY:
DO OVER ADOPTION

For this activity, please read the following example of a public online post that is seeking new adoptive families for the children described. Then answer the following questions. You can also see more examples of real posts on https://wiaa.org/2nd-chance-adoption /waiting-children/.

(Please remember that although these children are not real, hundreds of boys and girls have had similar ads placed on online public platforms that anyone can have access to.)

BERNICE DOE

Bernice is a kind, 10-year-old girl who was adopted domestically. She struggles with attachment and would do best in a home in which she is the youngest child, but she would ideally prefer a single-child household.

She strives with reinforcement and loves to earn tickets for extra screentime or recess at school. Bernice also loves animals, dolls, and crafts. She always makes sure her room is clean and puts away her toys nicely as well as her shoes.

KYLE DOE

Kyle is an energetic 10-year-old who was adopted internationally, but like many children who are looking for another adoptive home, he would do best in a home with a single parent and no other children. Kyle has spina bifida and is described by his parents as "loyal, kind, and active." He needs ongoing physical therapy and other services. He loves the color blue, hiking, reading, and blowing bubbles.

Kyle is very affectionate, loves to help around the house, and isn't shy when meeting new people. He does excellent when receiving 1:1 attention from an adult, enjoys body movement, and always wants to be involved with what is happening around him.

Adoption is a legal process so there will be costs associated with it. This adoption may qualify for some tax credit. To protect the privacy of our waiting children and their families, Do Over Adoptions does not share real names for our waiting children on the Internet. It is our policy to only share a snippet of a waiting child's details as well as the type of adoptive family we are looking for. If you fit the POSTED REQUIREMENTS, are home-study ready (or can be soon!), and are interested in adding this child to your family, please write to us for an honest, in-depth profile on the child, including medical, educational, and behavioral information, and learn the full story of why this child needs a secondary adoption.

Please share and like to get the word out on Facebook!

What are some safety concerns you have about this post?

How does this post make you feel? Please explain why you believe you feel this way.

What challenges do you think a family has to face to get to the point where they feel like this is the best option. Please add to the following list:

1. Safety of other children/adults in the home

2. Lack of resources for services

3.

4.

5.

Although it can be easy to sympathize with parents who feel that this is their best option, we need to remember the ramifications of rehoming and how that affects the child. Children who are rehomed are at greater risk of abuse, neglect, and additional trauma because the process has little oversight and their home life is disrupted. Typically, the largest contributing factors to rehoming are families who lack information to locate services they need and the cost of those services.[8]

Do you think the parents involved would have tried harder for a biological child? Why or why not?

What can adoptive parents do to prevent their adoption from getting to this point?

LEVEL UP Would you want your child sharing information about themselves on social media/the internet? Would you speak about your child in this manner or share information like this about them on the internet? Reflect on what you feel is the appropriate material/content to share about your child with others.

HISTORY OF ADOPTION

Do you know the history of adoption in and outside of the United States? If you are interested in adopting it is important to know some of the ethical issues that have impacted marginalized individuals and the harm that has been done along the way.

Here are some key moments in history that have shaped adoption industry.

The Baby Scoop Era

The *Baby Scoop Era* refers to the time between 1945 and 1971 when over 1.5 million unwed mothers were pressured into giving up their babies for adoption. During this time period, access to birth control and sex education were very limited and far behind where they are today; in some states, birth control was illegal for those who were unmarried. The girls and women who found themselves with unwanted pregnancies during this time period were pressured by social service agencies, their clergy, their family members, and society in general to give up their child for adoption. Adoption was seen as the only acceptable option; anything else led to shame for the unwed mother and the entire family, and often, ostracization. During this time, these women were told to stay quiet, move on, and forget what happened.[9]

Whether you are pro-choice or pro-life, it is essential that you look at the effects of restricting abortion and limiting a pregnant person's options. Please take some time to think about and answer the following questions:

- Considering the history of women and pregnant people in crisis, how can we better support such pregnant people now to prevent another Baby Scoop situation?

- What type of support is currently available for a pregnant person in need?

- What barriers are there to these support programs and networks?

- Without healthcare for all, how are pregnant people going to receive necessary prenatal, labor, and postnatal care?

- If a pregnant person doesn't have a support network, has limited funds, and is unhoused, how do you think that will impact their decision to place their child for adoption?

- How much money do you think it would take to support a family to keep them together?

Operation Babylift

Operation Babylift occurred in 1975 at the end of the Vietnam War when President Ford directed funds from foreign aid to fly around 2,000 orphans from South Vietnam to the United States. Many of these orphans were under two years old and had to be carried onto the plane. Dennis Traynor, the pilot of the first of these flights, had to crash land the cargo plane due to a malfunction that resulted in the death of 78 children and 50 adults. When the children eventually reached the United States, they were given new names, and since there was no passenger manifest, it has been difficult to trace the children.[10]

It has since been found that many of these children were not actually orphans; those who were fathered by American soldiers were thought to be in danger as the communists advanced in South Vietnam. At the time, Graham Martin, the American Ambassador in Vietnam, stated that the evacuation would help improve the American public opinion. President Ford used the opportunity to take advantage of the photos taken at the airport with airlifted children. Some saw this as an attempt to gain sympathy and approval for the war by showing the "saving" of orphans, but others felt that the orphans may not have needed saving at all and were perhaps lost and taken from their community and culture.[11] It was actually common practice at the time for poor families in Vietnam to place their children in orphanages if they could not care for them, but they still visited their children. Many children were adopted out of these orphanages, despite the lack of consent from their parents. Even though a case that expressed ethical concerns about Operation Babylift was brought to courts by Bay Area attorney Tom Miller, the case was dismissed, and the records were sealed.[12]

Baby Factories

In Nigeria, illegal shelters that are involved in exploiting young girls who have given birth to children for illegal adoption and trafficking are referred to as the *baby factories*. The continued prevalence of baby factories in Nigeria is often due to the high rates of poverty in the country and the constant demand for infant children by childless couples around the world. Adoption rings can make a lucrative profit off of this supply and demand. In baby factories, there are many cases of abuse of underaged girls who are used for child labor and are often forced to give birth to unwanted pregnancies; children born into these places can be used for child labor, as child soldiers, and even for prostitution. Young girls are often tricked into the factories by being promised help and support during their pregnancies. There have also been documented reports of young girls being kidnapped, impregnated, and held until they give birth.[13]

Nigeria is just one of several countries to engage in illegal and unethical practices, so it is very important for prospective adoptive parents who are interested in adoption (particularly international adoption) to do their due diligence in making sure everything is legal and appropriate.

Marshall Islands Trafficking Scandal

Hearing stories like these can be frightening and disheartening, and you may even think that you could never be part of something like illegal adoptions. But unfortunately, some adoption agencies are also involved in shady practices that use ethical gray areas and adoptive parents' desire for a baby to cloud their judgment.

Paul Petersen, a United States Republican and former politician, pleaded guilty in June of 2020 to human smuggling and various other charges related to an illegal adoption scheme in three states, in which he took advantage of women from the Marshall Islands. Originally, Petersen was charged with illegally paying women to come to the United States to give their babies up for adoption. This lasted for about three years and resulted in about seventy adoption cases in Utah, Arizona, and Arkansas. The women who were brought to Utah had little prenatal care, and their passports were taken once they arrived in the United States. Petersen pleaded guilty in Utah to one count of communications fraud and three counts of human smuggling, which are all felonies.[14] In December of 2020, he was sentenced to seventy-four months in federal prison for his illegal adoption scam, that the judge called a "get-rich-quick scheme . . . hidden behind the shiny veneer of a humanitarian operation."[15]

US Border Crisis

As of October of 2020, the government still had not found over 500 children who were separated from their parents during Trump's immigration crackdown at the United States and Mexican border. The ACLU stated that their efforts to reunite families have been hindered by incomplete government reports and difficult conditions in the children's native lands. Department of Homeland Security officials have said the government is working to reunite the children but have found that some parents do not want to claim their children because not claiming them allows the children to stay in the United States. Others hope to be reunited in the United States. Between July 2017 and June 2018, over 1,500 children were separated from their families, and by the time the district Judge Dana Sabraw issued a reunification order, many parents were unaccounted for.[16] In 2021 over 122,000 migrant children were taken into the custody of the United States; meanwhile in Texas officials created a new rule that shelters intended to house migrant children no longer need to be authorized with licenses to care for minors by the state. This means that those shelters are no longer subject to oversight, putting more children at risk.[17] Meanwhile advocates continue to try to reunite families, but often lawyers must rely on networking with nonprofit staff and human rights lawyers led by Justice in Motion, a group that is on the ground trying to track down families in El Salvador, Mexico, Honduras, and Guatemala. Such groups have had to pause their efforts due to the coronavirus.[18]

In 2018, US officials said that over 200 families that were separated at the US border remain ineligible for reunification or release. In addition, a major loophole in the system was found by the Associated Press that allowed state court judges (in Central America) to grant custody of migrant children to American families without notifying the child's parents, who are often deported hundreds of miles away. State courts often seal records in child custody cases, and the federal agencies involved in such immigration cases do not keep track of these records.[19]

Alexa was one such woman who was separated from her fifteen-month-old daughter and had to fight tooth and nail to get her back. Her daughter was placed in the United States foster care, run by the agency Bethany Christian Services, after they were separated at the border. This agency recently acknowledged that since the 1980s, some of the migrant children it was assigned were adopted by American families, despite the fact that foster families are not "allowed" to adopt migrant children.[20]

Roe v. Wade and Today

Now that the Supreme Court has overturned Roe v. Wade it is important to consider possible reasons behind such a decision like the need to provide a "domestic supply of infants."[21] When I spoke to a few women who work for Saving Our Sisters, an advocacy organization focusing on family preservation of pregnant persons in crisis, they said that the organization spends approximately $2,000 to help parents through a temporary crisis so they can parent.

When abortion is taken away, women are left with heartbreaking decisions. Before 2006, there was a ban on abortion in Colombia, and my birth mother placed not one, but three of her children for adoption. Centers that were framed to help women in need gave her accommodations while she was pregnant and some access to work programs, but they discharged her only days after she gave birth.

> NOTE Many people often hold the belief that adoption is the opposite of abortion when in fact parenting is the opposite of adoption. Abortion is a solution for someone who does not desire to be pregnant or when the pregnancy poses an imminent risk.

The cycle then repeated for my mother. People who are in these situations need more than just the Band-Aid of help that adoption allows. But if people who are pro-life aren't willing to give enough support to pregnant people in crisis, is that really pro-life? Or is that simply using someone until they no longer have what you want. In such cases, agencies make thousands upon thousands of dollars to "save" babies. As a US citizen, it's hard to see the right to an abortion stripped away just because some people believe that pregnant people should carry to term despite the consequences.

What about the parent's mental and physical health? What about the trauma of adoption for the child?

When I talk to my mother in Colombia and hear her sobs, I can't help but imagine how much different her life would have been if these centers were used to actually help women, not just for their own profit and the gain of adoptive parents. What if, instead, they put their efforts into stopping systemic issues that put people in these tough spots? When I researched adoption and abortion for my book, I found it interesting to see that adoption rates go down when abortion is legalized. If less stigma is associated with unwed parenthood, people are more likely to choose to parent.[22] So, as an adoptee, I think that if more of the right supports were in place, rather than for-profit adoption agencies, more first families would choose to parent their children in the long run. But I suppose that idea is not good for business.

ACTiViTY:
MiSSiNG FOSTER CHiLDREN

Every year, nearly 20,000 children go missing from foster care in the United States. For this activity, look up how many children go missing from foster care in at least two states and respond to the following questions:

1. Where do you think the children go?

2. How can we hold the system accountable?

ARTICLES TO READ:

- www.usatoday.com/story/opinion/columnist/2022/02/24 /children-disappear-foster-care-trafficking/6829115001/

- https://2b997067-e6f0-44b9-abf5-69867df2e6d3.usrfiles.com /ugd/2b9970_059b8c1746d64a588d8616fc27c3678b.pdf

- www.washingtonpost.com/nation/2022/05/23/missing-foster-care-children/

NOTE Those in foster care are also at increased risk for identity theft, which can leave them facing debt and other challenges even after they are out of the system. With their personal and identifying information being passed around within agencies, between caseworkers and potentially multiple families, foster care youth are at increased risk of being taken advantage of in this way.

RED FLAGS ADOPTIVE PARENTS CAN LOOK FOR

Ask yourself the following questions for each agency you are investigating. If the information is not easily available on their website, do not hesitate to contact them via email or ask an employee. You can use the outline in the following activity if you need help.

- How does the adoption agency talk about expectant (birth) parents? Is the agency working to protect their rights?

- Does the agency call the pregnant parent a "birth" parent before the baby has been born?

- How does the agency interact with expectant parents? Read the section of their website aimed at expectant parents.

- How does the agency get in contact with expectant parents considering adoption?

- How does the agency handle the rights of birth fathers? Do they encourage mothers not to name the fathers?

- Does the agency support family preservation first?

- Does the agency encourage the expectant parent to spend time with her baby after giving birth, even if adoption papers were signed?

- Are the agency's licensing requirements up to date?

- Does the agency offer shorter wait times for higher fees? Do they participate in race-based pricing?

- Do you feel pressure from the agency to act now?

- What does the agency do if the birth parent decides against adoption and chooses to parent? Do they provide the pregnant person with resources?

NONPROFIT FINANCIALS

Nonprofit agencies are required to make their financials public record; these can be viewed on websites like Guidestar.org. When looking at the forms, make sure you are asking yourself the following questions:

- Where is my money going?

- How much of my money is going toward fundraising?

- What is the average executive compensation for this agency?

- What post-adoption services does this agency provide for adoptees and birth parents?

- Is this agency investing in adoptees and birth parents by providing education, services, and therapy?

SOME NONPROFIT FINANCIALS TO EXPLORE:

- www.holtinternational.org/wp-content/uploads/2022/04/IRS-Form-990 -Holt-International-2021.pdf

- https://bethany.org/media/about-us/2021-parent-bethany-christian -serivces.pdf

- www.diakon.org/about-us/annual-report/

ACTIVITY:
EMAIL OUTLINE

Have you been concerned that an adoption agency that you are working with has some ethical concerns? Use this template letter to begin a conversation with the agency and those in charge.

Hello _____,

    I hope you are having a great week!

    My name is _____, and I am interested in working with your adoption agency. I have been doing some research (with my partner), and we have a few questions before we move forward. We are doing our best as potential adoptive parents to make sure we adopt in an ethical way that also supports birth parents and family preservation. After looking at your website (or talking to _____), we would love to learn more about how _____ approaches adoption.

    Could you please point me to where I could find the answers for my questions? I can also email them over if that would work best.

    Thank you for your help.

Best,

_____

LEVEL UP Challenge yourself to go and meet face to face with staff at an agency. Notice if staff members provide differing answers, are unable to answer or evade questions, or provide answers that seem rehearsed or too similar. Notice the staff members' level of comfort with you asking the difficult questions.

CHAPTER 2 REFLECTION QUESTIONS

- What surprised you the most in this chapter? What concerns you the most?

- What do you plan on doing to help adoption become more ethical?

3

IDENTITY

I was around six years old when I first faced the fact that I had brown skin and most of the kids I went to school with were white. This made me stand out, and I distinctly remember how a girl in my class told me I couldn't play with her because she thought I was Black. I looked down at my hands and up at her face and back down again, confused.

That day, I remember going home and asking my mom why that little girl said what she said and why I looked different. My mother reassured me that it meant nothing and not to mind anything anyone said about my appearance, but despite what she said, the girl's comments continued to bother me. From that day foreword, I looked at my face in the mirror, picking apart the differences I saw between myself and my family, friends, and community.

As an adult looking back at those memories, what I find interesting is that I was just a child when I realized that my skin color affected how the world saw me and how I saw myself. It was something that othered me in a primarily white environment, and those around me who loved me didn't know how to address those differences; it became something taboo.

This is why, in this chapter, we will be discussing racial and ethnic identity and the importance that developing a healthy racial identity has for transracial adoptees. We will dig into identity development, activities that will help you support children of color, and questions that will help you learn the importance identity has for adopted children of color.

To start, think about the following:

- Did you parents discuss race with you as a child?

- What is your main motivation for adopting a child from another culture?

- What do you most look forward to about adopting transracially?

- How do you think adopting a child will impact you and your family?

- What are your extended families' views of transracial adoption?

- Have you planned to discuss transracial adoption with them?

- Do you have anti-racist babysitters lined up who can care for your child while you are not around?

ARE TRANSRACIAL ADOPTEES THE SOLUTION TO RACISM?

When it first became popular for white parents to adopt children of color, families were advised to raise the adoptees as if they were white. This recommendation was based on the idea that recognizing racial differences would negatively affect development. Later research has shown that transracial adoptees are not exempt from prejudice and racial stress simply because they were raised within a white family.[1] In an ideal world, children would not face any discrimination. Unfortunately, we live in a world that emphasizes our physical appearance, and often that includes our race and ethnicity.

Racial prejudice is a pressing issue. By age three, children can identify racial groups; by ages six to eight, children can consistently classify others by race. Despite this, many adopted parents raised children with a colorblind mentality. *Colorblindness*, also known as the *colorblind racial ideology*, is the widely held belief that skin color does not play a role in interpersonal interactions and institutional policies and/or practices.[2] As a woman of color, it is hard for me to understand why so many adoptive parents take a colorblind perspective when race plays a significant role in so many things.

EFFECTS ON MENTAL HEALTH

Research has begun documenting the harmful effects of racism on the mental and physical health of people of color. Now we know that these effects can lead to higher rates of depression, anxiety, suicidal ideation, even obesity and cardiovascular disease.[3] Some studies show that negative mental health symptoms can appear when people of color are treated like second-class citizens, when they are exoticized, or when they have their experiences invalidated. Racism is often a stressor that elicits coping responses as well as physical and mental stress responses that can contribute to negative health outcomes.

Racial minorities can also experience a trauma response that can result in hypervigilance and hypersensitivity to certain social situations that are triggering. In addition, racism can contribute to negative effects on mental health when people of color internalize negative racial stereotypes that harm their self-worth. Institutional racism contributes to experiencing the effects of chronic stressors and poor living conditions.[4] The lack of a quality support network and the limited number of health professionals and therapists of color can contribute a significant barrier to mental health access.[5]

> NOTE Trauma responses include fight, flight, freeze, and fawn and describe the ways in which an individual's system responds to a perceived threat. These occur at an unconscious level when the amygdala has been activated.

In 2016, approximately 85 percent of therapists in the United States were white. Only 4 percent were Black, and another 4 percent were Hispanic.[6] If you want to seek out a therapist who is also adoption competent, you will find very few, and those who are available may not be in your network. This creates a huge discrepancy in the quality and frequency of care people of color are able to receive, which is why it should not be surprising that racism is a significant risk factor of negative mental health outcomes.[7] Please go to Chapter 5 for more information about mental health.

ACTiViTY:
GAUGE YOUR NORMAL

Describe a BIPOC person in your life.

Describe a white person in your life.

Now look at both examples. When you describe a friend/coworker/stranger, do you use race as a descriptor? Or do you try to avoid it? Why or why not?

LEVEL UP What purpose does using someone's race as a descriptor serve? Reflect on how family members, caregivers, and teachers described individuals of different races as you were growing up. Is this a learned behavior? The way you refer to individuals will be picked up on by your children. What's learned can be unlearned.

CENTERING WHITENESS

Although from a young age I understood that my identity was different from those around me, it surprised me to learn that my parents didn't really think of race in the same way that I did. It was only after I brought up the topic during summer break after a semester of cross-cultural psychology that my parents even considered that they were part of a racial group.

In fact, I remember the shocked expressions on their faces as we discussed how they were technically "white" even though they focused on being Italian and Portuguese. Initially they became frustrated when I suggested this and even rejected the idea that this label applied to them. Then they immediately denied that whiteness came with any sort of privilege.

It wasn't until months later, after reading more essays about identity, that I was introduced to the idea of whiteness being the default and its impact on how everyone interacts with one another. When we center whiteness, it can lead to the idea that white is ideal or "normal," which can make it difficult for BIPOC who have to function in environments that automatically cater to their white counterparts.

A lot of the time people will describe someone with certain descriptors like tall, funny, or skinny. But if that person is BIPOC, often people add descriptors that either directly refer to race (Black, Asian, and the like) or that suggest the person's race in a roundabout way. However, if the person being described happens to be white, race is often left out of the conversation. In other words, it is implied that the person is white unless otherwise specified because whiteness is so often centered.

INEQUALITIES INFLUENCED BY CENTERING WHITENESS

The following are some inequalities that can happen when whiteness is the default.

HEALTHCARE BIAS

- Mortality rate for Black women and persons of color who give birth is higher.[8]

- Healthcare professionals have difficulty diagnosing children with certain conditions that appear different on darker skin tones because they are taught primarily with images of white patients.[9]

- BIPOC patients are thought to have higher pain tolerances.[10]

- Black infant mortality rates are twice that of non-Hispanic white infants.[11]

- Black people are more likely to die from a stroke or heart disease before the age of seventy-five than their white counterparts.[12]

- Latinx and Black people also have higher rates of diabetes, tuberculosis, HIV, and preventable hospitalizations.[13]

BIASED TESTING IN SCHOOLS

- Educators across the US have often criticized the use of standardized testing, in part due to its history of bias against Black, Latino, Indigenous, and Asian children.[14]

- Standardized testing is based on a history of eugenics that believed in the superiority of the Nordic race group and warned against immigrants.[15]

- Schools that place high stakes on standardized testing ignore inequalities in education and environment that affect scores.[16] For example:

  ▶ Higher rates of Black males in special education

  ▶ English language learners

  ▶ Lower income families who do not have the funds for tutors, extra classes, and can't take time off work to study

  ▶ BIPOC students with disabilities who are less likely to receive services

NOTE Across my practice I see adopted children struggling greatly in school due to their nervous system being unable to attain a baseline of safety. Teachers and school staff often have limited insight into the complex needs of adoptees, which can lead to chronic triggering of attachment wounds.

EUROCENTRIC BEAUTY STANDARDS AT SCHOOL AND THE WORKPLACE

- Workplace discrimination against natural Black hair[17]

- Bias against Black and Brown bodies in the same clothing as their white counterparts[18]

- Colorism in the workplace[19]

ACTIVITY:
VOCABULARY AND TERMINOLOGY

If you are not familiar with them, please look up and write down the definitions of the following terms before digging into the rest of this chapter.

Racial Imposter Syndrome:

Racial legitimacy:

Code-switching:

Implicit bias:

Passing or white passing:

Becoming an (antiracism) ally:

HOW CAN WE COMBAT SYSTEMIC RACISM IN ADOPTION?

Cultural socialization—the way parents address racial and ethnic issues within the family and how they communicate customs, cultural values, and behaviors to their children.

In transracial adoptive families, culturally socializing your child means transmitting the child's birth culture to them, which is important in order for them to create a strong ethnic identity and overall well-being for themselves.[20] But doing this is not as clear-cut a process as it is in same-race families. This may be because white Americans are less likely to consider themselves part of a racial group, which can contribute to the difficulty they have recognizing the privilege in their lives, and it can make it easier for white adoptive parents to minimize or even deny the significance of race in our society.[21]

Parents who subscribe to less colorblindness seem to engage more with post-adoption support groups and cultural activities and even speak about racism with their adopted children. However, studies show that it is best to participate in cultural socialization in addition to engaging in racial awareness. Parents who are willing to put in the extra effort to learn about racism and discrimination are more likely to positively contribute to their child's ethnic development and well-being.[22]

When adoptive parents find it difficult to believe adoptees when we try to share our experiences with racism, it can cause conflicts in our relationships. As transracial adoptees, we are in a unique position to be deeply involved in our adoptive parent's majority culture while also being part of a minority culture that is subjected to discrimination and racism. Adoptees may find it painful to navigate the space between these two very different cultures while trying to fit in with each, especially if they don't have a definitive way to merge the two without repercussions and difficulty. It can be painful to see our adoptive parents' jealousy when we express interest in our birth culture. This may make us feel guilty, and at the same time, we may experience overwhelming shame that we don't know our birth culture well enough.

The following are some ways to practice cultural socialization.

ACTIVITY:
COMBATTING SYSTEMIC RACISM

NURTURE

Look for and maintain a strong connection with your child's BIPOC community. Start by researching community events in your neighborhood (i.e., festivals, camps, etc.) and make the time to bring your family to them. Encourage your child's interest in food, music, and other ties to their culture and make sure you show the same joy and interest.

EXPLORE

What are some places/activities your family can explore this month? Use the space provided to brainstorm, and start making a list of twelve activities to do this year that will help your children connect to their culture.

Please remember that exploring a primarily BIPOC event can be stressful for adoptees. We can have worries about not fitting in, of standing out, or of being asked intrusive questions. Before setting out, expand on the following ways you can make your child feel supported and safe so they can explore. Feel free to add more ideas in addition to these.

1. **Open communication:** Have a conversation about fears and goals for the event. What are some questions you can ask your child?

2. **Role-play experiences:** Pretend that you are at the event and have your child walk through certain scenarios they would face in real life. (i.e., ordering food at a restaurant, learning a new dance). Write down some ideas to try.

DESTIGMATIZE RACE

Create a space in which race is just a normal part of the conversation. Making daily affirmations that Black and Brown skin is beautiful and talking openly about racism can help adoptees develop a healthy racial identity. Validate your adopted children's feelings about any discrimination they may experience in their life and build up their self-esteem.

W IN WHITE

There are those who argue that we should capitalize the W in white just as we do for Black, Indigenous, Asian, and Latinx/e. Write an argument for and against this capitalization. Feel free to research your side and the counterargument and write three to five sentences for both sides.

For capitalization:

Against capitalization:

REFLECT

Encourage your child to explore questions about race and their identities. Search for adoption support groups and transracial adoptee mentoring where they can learn first-hand from a peer that has been through the process and knows the nuances of the journey intimately. Think about how your community, your child's school, and your family are made up of people of various cultures, and think about how that impacts how your child of color walks through their world and how their journey is different from your own.

UMBRELLA OF PRIVILEGE

Another unique complication for transracial adoptees is that when we are with our white adoptive family, we experience an umbrella of white privilege that protects us, but the second we are out on our own and do not have our adoptive families around to vouch for us, we lose that protection. At this point, we must be prepared for the social implications of being a BIPOC. If we are raised in homes that promote colorblindness, we can be left vulnerable and unprepared for the reality of our position in a country built on systemic racism.

NOTE Many transracial adoptees I have worked with notice that they are treated differently when they are not with their adoptive parents. Instances that can highlight this are when teens go to college, when they are in environments where no one knows their adoptive parents, on job interviews, and during transitions to new grade levels.

ACTIVITY:
ANALYZING YOUR UMBRELLA

In the center of this umbrella, write down ways your child has benefited from your white privilege when in your presence. Think about how people interact with your child or teen at church or at the grocery store versus when they are alone. On the outside of the umbrella, draw a few raindrops and for each drop, write down experiences your child can have when they don't have the benefit of your white privilege.

REAL-LIFE IMPLICATIONS OF RACE

How do children develop a strong sense of self? We know from research that how kids develop is based on nature or genes and also on nurture, or how their environment shapes them. Research has shown that transracial adoptees may withhold sharing experiences with racism for several reasons: they prefer to fit in with their adoptive family, they are acting in self-preservation, or they have experienced past unresponsiveness from their adoptive parents who have avoided discussing the topic of discrimination.[23]

For children of color, developing an ethnic or racial identity is a vital milestone, so let's talk about it. Why is it important?

Children with a strong racial or ethnic identity are more likely to have positive self-esteem, a healthy social network, fewer depressive symptoms, higher levels of academic achievement and motivation, and less drug use.[24]

ACTiViTY:
CREATE A PLAN TO DEAL WiTH RACiSM

How can you prepare your child to cope with racism? For this activity, please ask your child if they have experienced any type of racism. Encourage them to share when they are ready to and make sure you provide a safe place where their feelings are validated. Look at the following list and use it as a way to launch and expand on this conversation.

The following are struggles transracial adoptees can face when they don't have a strong racial identity:

- Not knowing how to cope with racism

- Being unprepared for the nuances of interacting with police

- Not fitting in with peers of the same race and not knowing cultural norms

- Disliking of their physical appearance

Just as families prepare for fires in their home or for a natural disaster, adoptive families need to make a plan to deal with racism. A time will come when your child is exposed to racism by a beloved family member or a family friend, and it is important to prepare for such an occasion before you think you need to.

Here are some questions to ask yourself:

- Am I willing to call out racist jokes?

- Am I willing to keep people who are unwilling to change out of my family's life?

- What would I say to a beloved family member who called my child a slur in public as a joke or even as a bad attempt at a compliment?

- How will I approach a situation in which my child comes to me and says my sibling (their aunt) made fun of their eyes or performed some other microaggression?

- Am I willing to confront and shut down racism anywhere and immediately?

- Am I willing to do this in public? Or just at home?

NOTE Questions/comments regarding your multiracial family will inevitably come up. The W.I.S.E. Up! curriculum sponsored by C.A.S.E., the Center for Adoption Support and Education (https://adoptionsupport.org/w-s-e-giving -adopted-kids-simple-tools-answer-tough-questions/) is a helpful tool for fami- lies. It empowers children and teens who have been adopted or who are in foster care to implement limits and boundaries with sharing information about them- selves, and it provides choices for how a child/family can respond to others' questions or comments.

IDENTITY AND MEDIA

When talking about identity development, it is important to consider the media that our children and families consume. What they are exposed to online, on TV, and in movies can shape how transracially adopted children view themselves, and it can impact their self-esteem.

Colorblind Casting

Because whiteness has been the default for so long, there is some backlash when things start to change. For example, historically Hollywood has been a white-dominated industry and even today, with diversity on the rise, Hollywood still has issues with col- orism and stereotyping characters in harmful ways. But one distinctive problem that I would like to discuss is colorblind casting: the idea that directors should not consider race when casting various roles. Although at a glance this can seem like a great idea to further diversify this industry and create more representation for BIPOC, the problem is that there is a huge double standard in the movie industry; it supports and pays for white actors to play BIPOC characters, meanwhile BIPOC actors who play tradition-ally white characters receive a huge backlash.

One influential example was when the live action *Little Mermaid* cast Halle Bailey, a Black singer and actress, as Ariel. For those who are unfamiliar with the movie, Ariel is typically portrayed as a white mermaid with vibrant red hair and blue eyes. In 2019, Bailey was announced as the lead, and the internet irrupted in hatred and anger that Disney would dare to cast the fictional character as a Black woman. Many of the critics tried to pass it off as it being unrealistic for a Black person to have red hair (although rare, some Black people have red hair) and threatened to stop supporting the movie because of "white erasure."[25]

Although criticism of a film is normal and even healthy, in this case we need to note that people are trying to pass their comments off as a critique of creative preferences, when in reality, it is blatant racism when people state the importance of a fictional character (i.e., a mermaid) looking a certain way when their race/ethnicity have no bearing on the actual role.

But when the opposite happens, and a BIPOC character is played by a white actor or actress, the actor is often subject to less criticism. We see this all the time with famous roles by actors such as Scarlett Johansson, who played the role of an Asian character Major Motoko Kusanagi in the 2017 film *Ghost in the Shell*, and many others.

How do you think your BIPOC child would feel after hearing/seeing such com-ments online or in person by those in their community?

ACTIVITY:
CRITIC'S CHOICE

Research an actor from a film or TV show who played a role written for a different race—either a white actor playing a role originally written as BIPOC, or a BIPOC actor playing a role originally written as white. Then answer the following questions.

What would you say to your child if they shared something negative a person said about a character being played by a Black actress?

How could you support your child in that moment?

Why are most criticisms of white actors valid in some way?

NOTE If you hear your child say something disparaging about themselves (regarding race or something else), your immediate reaction may be to tell them the opposite or talk them out of feeling that way. Instead of jumping to shift their perspective or change their answer, focus on just being curious about why those comments may be coming up and hold space.

ACTIVITY:
DECOLONIZING YOUR BOOKSHELF

What percentage of traditionally published books do you think are by white authors?

What percentage of books that are traditionally published do you think are by BIPOC authors? Please fill out the following pie chart with your guesses.

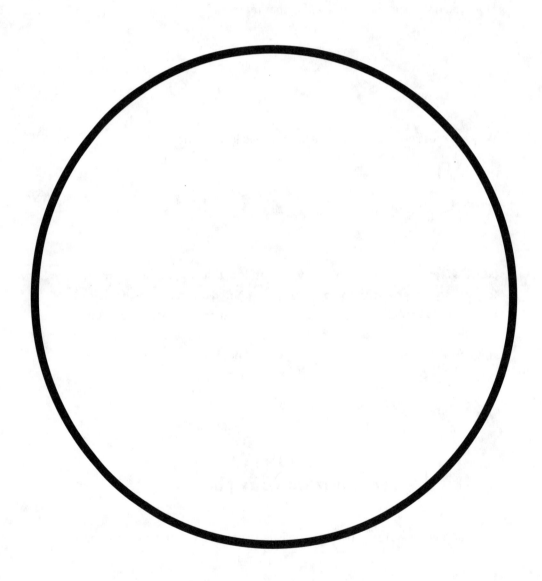

Take inventory of all of the literature in your home and tally here how my books are by white, Black, Indigenous, and other persons of color. If you find that more than half of your books are by white authors, now is a great time to purchase new books by more #ownvoice authors. #*Ownvoice* books are written by people from marginalized groups about their own experiences/perspectives.

CHILDREN'S BOOKS BY

_____ Black authors

_____ Latinx authors

_____ Asian authors

_____ Indigenous authors

_____ White authors

ADULT BOOKS BY:

_____ Black authors

_____ Latinx authors

_____ Asian authors

_____ Indigenous authors

_____ White authors

Eurocentric Standards in Media

When we look at publishing or the Hollywood film industry, we can see the heavy influence of Eurocentric standards and the visible backlash when the production or publication goes against the norms. According to the Lee & Low Books 2019 Survey of Diversity in Publishing, 76 percent of publishing staff, review journal staff, and literary agents are white. A fraction self-report as Asian/Native Hawaiian/Pacific Islander (7 percent); Hispanic/Latino/Mexican (6 percent); Black/African American (5 percent); and biracial/multiracial (3 percent). Native Americans and Middle Easterners each comprise less than 1 percent of publishing staff.[26]

These figures are significant, particularly if we look at the race/ethnicity of authors who are published. According to a sample of around 7,000 books published by Simon & Shuster, Penguin Random House, Doubleday, HarperCollins, and Mac-Millan, only 11 percent of books were written by authors of color.[27]

Importance of Racial Mirrors in Media

If most of the media we consume is created by majority white creators, then the material we are consuming does not provide BIPOC people with accurate representation. This can lead to hurtful stereotypes and can lead to BIPOC people feeling like their stories and lives don't matter as much.

When I was a little girl, I found it very difficult growing up without knowing or being around anyone who really looked like I did. One example that stuck with me until recently was the lack of representation in Disney princesses. When I was just a kid, the closest princess I had who "looked" like me was Belle, from *Beauty and the Beast*, because she had dark hair and eyes. The older I got, the more I realized that she was a poor substitute for a mirror, and it made me feel like I wasn't good enough, like my friends and family who were represented.

But in 2022, things changed completely when Disney finally depicted a Colombian character that I could relate to in its movie *Encanto*. Mirabel has warm brown skin, wild, curly, black hair, and is petite just like me. At twenty-nine years old, I finally had that representation in the media that I had craved, and it was beautiful. It warmed a part of my soul and made me feel worthy.

Of course, as an adult I have worked on my self-esteem and am not as reliant on media as I was growing up. But when you are a person of color and have to see books and movies that often illustrate negative stereotypes about your people, it can make you question your worth, particularly when you are part of a family that doesn't look like you, especially if you live in a community that is mostly white too.

WHY ARE RACIAL MIRRORS IMPORTANT?

- They help children feel seen and validated.

- Positive role models help children build self-esteem.

- They can help children learn empathy by imagining themselves in others' shoes more easily.

- Their presence provides openings for tough conversations.

- They can encourage children to dream big.

CAN YOU EXPAND ON THE REASONS WHY? CAN YOU THINK OF
ANY MORE REASONS?

WHAT HAPPENS WHEN MIRRORS ARE MISSING?

▶ Children may show a decreased interest in school.

▶ Children are less likely to read for pleasure.

▶ Lack of mirrors can impact self-esteem negatively.

NOTE Common negative beliefs that are built due to the lack of racial mirrors
include these:

- I'm not good enough.

- I'm invisible.

- I don't matter.

- No one understands.

- I'm not valuable.

- I'm bad.

WHAT ARE SOME OTHER PROBLEMS THAT CAN OCCUR WHEN
CHILDREN GROW UP WITHOUT MIRRORS?

WHAT ARE SOME OF YOUR FAVORITE SHOWS WITH RACIAL MIR-
RORS THAT REPRESENT THE FOLLOWING RACES/ETHNICITIES?

Black

Indigenous

Asian

Latinx

MICROAGGRESSIONS AND THEIR IMPACT

Transracial adoption is considered the most visible of all adoptions, and as transracial
adoptees, we often feel more conscious of our race because of our parents' visible
differences from us. Transracial adoptees have unique experiences as we develop our
identity; together, these are referred to as the *transracial adoption paradox*. More specifically, this term refers to the set of contradictory experiences faced by adoptees who
are members of racial minority groups raised by a white majority culture.[28]

> NOTE Exposure to chronic microaggressions can result in as much adverse
> impact as a single intense traumatic experience.

The research on the relationship between mental health and discrimination of transracial adoptees is still in the beginning stages, but in 2015, a study did find that experiences with discrimination are associated with substance use issues, anxiety, and even cheating.[29] Because there are links between racial discrimination and the health of adoptees, both physical and mental, the adoption community must become more open to listening to the experiences of adult adoptees who are willing to share their struggles with the aim of educating and preparing adoptive parents for what their children may go through.

The traditional thought process is that racism involves overt acts of hate against BIPOC, but the truth is that racism often appears in more nuanced ways. In addition, research has shown that white Americans struggle to accept the more nuanced divisions of racism, possibly because they feel implicated in their use.[30] More subtle acts of racism are commonly known as *microaggressions*, which can also be broken up into three forms: microassaults, microinsults, and microinvalidations.

Microassaults are the more overt forms of discrimination; they can take the form of either verbal or nonverbal attacks or even avoidant behaviors.[31] Common examples include a white person crossing the street to avoid a BIPOC, clutching their purse on an elevator when a person of color stands next to them, or when a white employee pays more attention to a BIPOC customer and follows them around the store. When this happens to transracial adoptees, and then our white parents join us, the employee suddenly finds it no longer necessary to follow us.

Microinsults are insensitive statements or actions that put down a person's racial identity.[32] Microinsults that people of color experience are statements such as "Oh, you're pretty for a Black/Asian/Indigenous girl," or "I thought you'd be better at math because you are Asian."

Microinvalidations are more common for adoptees and occur when a person negates or denies the feelings and experiences of a person of color.[33] Transracial adoptees often experience microinvalidations when we share experiences with racism with our adoptive families that are then denied. We may be told "I didn't mean it *that* way" or "you think everything is racist."

THREE WAYS WHITE PARENTS CAN BE BETTER ALLIES

1. Engage in consistent anti-racism work, not just when something pops up in the news.

2. Use your voice to address bias and support BIPOC at school or work.

3. Sit in your discomfort and learn from mistakes.

NOTE Those who experience trauma can be highly sensitive to words being backed up with actions. Follow-through is critical. Being an ally for any marginalized group requires you to act, which can increase their feelings of trust and safety.

ACTIVITY:
HOW TO EXPLORE RACISM WITH CHILDREN

What are some actions that you can take while exploring racism with your children? Please read each section and brainstorm how you can incorporate these tips into your family's day-to-day life.

LIMIT EXPOSURE TO VIOLENCE

Just because a certain news event involves BIPOC individuals does not mean that it is appropriate to show it to a child of color. You can discuss events in an age-appropriate conversation and encourage conversation and questions without exposing children to extremely violent videos that can deepen trauma.

Choose a news event and write down ways you can share age-appropriate information with a

- Child

- Teen

- Adult

FOCUS ON SAFETY

Learning about racism and the dangers it can pose for BIPOC individuals is important, but it can also increase feelings of fear and hopelessness. Remind children of actions that they can take to keep themselves and their friends/family safe and remember to talk about empowering stories as well.

What are some actions that your child can take to keep them safe in public?

- Removing hoodie when walking outside or in public

-

-

CONFUSION IS NORMAL

Children who are transracially adopted, biracial, and/or multiracial may have difficulty understanding their own racial identity. Remind them that they have time to figure out how they are most comfortable identifying and that you will support their journey along the way by providing them with books, movies, and mentors to walk them through it.

What are some films or books that you can share with your child?

FIND SAFE AND AGE-APPROPRIATE ACTION

With more information easily available at the touch of a few buttons, the younger generation has shown an amazing desire to advocate for change and action. Support your children and teens who want to make a difference and explore ways for them and the rest of the family to get involved.[34]

What are some age-appropriate actions your child can take in their community?

- Child

- Teen

- Adult

NOTE When a child sees racial violence on TV, in the newspaper, in video games, and so on, especially before they are developmentally able to understand it, the child may feel less safe.

IMPORTANCE OF BEAUTY AND HYGIENE

When it comes to beauty and hygiene for Black and Brown children, it is not simply about looking good to look good. Hair has deep roots with culture and identity in the Black community, and it is important to remember that hair care is a necessity for transracially adopted children so they can look *and* feel good.

Although I am no expert, I feel that it is important to include this section to point parents in the direction of Black creators who provide classes and trainings for adoptive parents of Black children. I also consulted my sister-in-law, Amanda Richards, who is a licensed esthetician and a lead esthetician at one of the most advanced facial bars in New York City, Silver Mirror Facial Bar. As a woman of color, from experience, I know that my skin needs more moisture, but I reached out to Amanda because I was really interested in learning the ins and outs of skincare professionally, especially for

BIPOC clients. Her mission is to make skincare effective, approachable, and accessible to everyone, and I'm excited to share some of her expertise here.

What do estheticians learn about BIPOC skincare?

When working on BIPOC clients, I have learned it is not only important to be mindful of how you treat their skin, but also it is important to educate your client on the best practices they can utilize when taking care of their skin.

BIPOC people have more melanin in their skin. Melanin is what gives our skin pigment. This means that their skin can also hyperpigment much easier when the skin is damaged. So it is important to be mindful of this so you can properly acclimate the skin to stronger treatments when you are working on darker skin tones.

Do BIPOC children need sunscreen?

Yes, BIPOC children need sunscreen. Sunscreen is intended to prevent UV damage to the skin cell. Melanin helps to protect the DNA of your skin cell from damage from the sun's UV rays, but it is not enough protection to solely rely on. You need to support your skin's protective barrier with sunscreen to prevent damage that could lead to hyperpigmentation, premature aging, and skin cancer.

Why do darker skin tones tend to need more moisture?

Darker skin tones typically have higher oil production but lower ceramides levels, so people with darker skin are more prone to transepidermal water loss and getting dehydrated.

What are the three hygiene and beauty tips you can recommend for parents of BIPOC children?

- Have open conversations about how skincare is part of self-care and that it's important to understand what is best for their skin and how to make their skincare routine manageable at a young age.

- Educate yourself about the differences in darker skin tones and the proper professional and at-home treatments to use.

- Always be empathetic about struggles children experience with their skin at a young age.

HAIRCARE AND SKINCARE

When it comes to skincare and haircare, it is important to remember that Black and Brown children often need more moisturizing products and have different cultural norms in their communities, like using a washcloth, wearing a bonnet, or washing their legs. It is important for white parents to do the work: they must teach their children how to care for their skin and hair and provide them with additional resources if they need more help. Here are some articles and videos to get you started.

Additional Resources for Hair Care

ARTICLES

- "Hair Love: The Evolution of Hair Acceptance + Discrimination in the Black Experience," by Ashleigh Williams, https://tinyurl.com/2xkkdy2w

- "40 Best Hair Products from Black-Owned Brands for Every Type and Texture," by Brian Underwood and Jane Burnett, https://tinyurl.com/4ks98ecm

- "6 Things Everyone Should Know about Black Hair History," by Nikki Fox, https://tinyurl.com/6rftuzea

YOUTUBE VIDEOS

- "Teaching Adoptive Parents to Care for Natural Hair," https://youtu.be/nWxwVLm1XD4

- "Multicultural Family Hair Wash Day," 2022, https://youtu.be/VAcoGtIJQzw

- "Our Mother/Daughter Hairstyles + How I Take Care of My Toddler's Hair," https://youtu.be/F4AyuQtDTTc

- "The Tangled History of Black Hair Discrimination in the US," https://youtu.be/KCh-AeU-o_4

WEBSITES

- "Hair Care with Heart," Styles 4 Kidz, https://www.styles4kidz.org

- Tutus & Tennis Shoes, https://tinyurl.com/5n7wcsw6

BLACK HAIR CARE TIPS

- Take a hair class by a Black transracial adoptee or Black person who offers education for white adoptive parents.

- Visit a Black beauty supply store.

- Take males to a barber regularly.

- Support Black-owned businesses.

- Avoid classes run by white "experts" unless you have exhausted every other option.

SUGGESTED ITEMS TO PURCHASE

- Bonnets

- Satin- or silk-lined pillows

- Satin- or silk-lined hoodies or hats

- Healthy Roots doll

Black Skincare Resources

- "How to Care for Skin of Color, According to Black and Brown Dermatologists," by Joseph Lamour, https://tinyurl.com/y8jhcwbz

- "This Instagram Account Is Fighting to Make Dermatology Less White," by A. Rochaun Meadows-Fernandez, https://tinyurl.com/2zrjc67n

- "Skin Cancer in People of Color," American Academy of Dermatology, https://tinyurl.com/mrbw5azh

- "The Skin Care Industry Is Failing People of Color," by Rita Omokha, https://tinyurl.com/2p9xrdz4

Suggested Items to Purchase

- Sunscreen without a white cast

  ▸ Black Girl Sunscreen

  ▸ Neutrogena Hydro Boost, Water Gel Lotion

- ▶ CeraVe Hydrating Sunscreen

- ▶ Vanicream Broad-Spectrum Sunscreen

- ▶ Supergoop Unseen Sunscreen

- ▶ Wander Beauty Pack Up and Glow Sunscreen

- Lotion with cocoa butters or oils that nourish

  - ▶ Palmer's Cocoa Butter

  - ▶ Gold Bond Ultimate Radiance Renewal

  - ▶ Sunny Isle Lavender Whipped Shea Butter

  - ▶ Jergens Wet Skin Body Moisturizer

DNA TESTING

DNA testing is a controversial topic in the adoption community. Some people are really for it, and some are extremely against it due to privacy concerns.

Many adoptees, particularly those of us who had closed adoptions, often reach a point in our lives when we consider DNA testing by companies like 23andMe or Ancestry.com. The promise of concrete knowledge about our race/ethnicity, as well as possible connections to close biological relatives, is often too tempting for us to resist. Trying to establish a family medical history is also a driving factor for many adoptees; I wanted to find out any medical information I could about my birth family. Using testing companies like this is often the most affordable and easily accessible option that we have.

In a *closed adoption* the adoptive family and birth family share little or no contact with one another, and identifying information from the birth family typically remains confidential. Non-identifying information that is often provided to adoptive parents includes the date and place of the adoptee's birth, the age of the birth parents, and a general physical description (i.e., eye and hair color), race/ethnicity/religion of birth parents, educational level and occupation of biological parents, and the reason the child was placed.[35] Many adoptees in closed adoptions have access to little to no medical information other than basic information about their health at birth; other adoptees may have one or two lines of information that a social worker was able to ask the birth mother before the adoption was finalized.

Things to Consider

The reasons that adoptees may desire a DNA search can vary from wanting medical information to learning about their ancestry/nationality to wanting to find biological relatives. Although such searches can open many doors, you may want to consider some things before taking tests with such companies.

For example, not only might your private information be shared, but you also might uncover some long-buried family secrets. For example, a person may take a DNA test expecting one result only to find out new information about their race and ethnicity. This can be shocking to learn after many years of growing up with a different identity. It is also important to remember that there are some barriers to access. For instance, tests can be expensive and may only be accessible in certain states and countries. In addition, not all tests provide the same information, and some platforms are easier to use than others. When considering genetic testing, keep these factors in mind before deciding to move forward.

Adoptees should also make sure they don't have false expectations. Having some answers about your DNA won't necessarily fix everything, nor should you hope that you will find close birth relatives immediately once your results are in. For years after taking a 23andMe test, I held my breath every time I received an email stating that new DNA matches had been found, only to be disappointed when I found that they were distant cousins who had no information about my birth mother.

It is also important to note that results from at-home DNA kits can vary greatly. Ethnicity at a regional level is pretty accurate, but more specific levels of analysis are less precise. Health information should also be taken with a grain of salt because false-positive results for the BRCA1 or BRCA2 gene mutations are not uncommon. That said, your results, in conjunction with any history you know about your birth family, can help you make medical decisions down the line.[36] According to a certified genetic counselor, DNA testing from consumer testing companies is often just a good place to start if you're interested in discovering more information about your genetic risks. It can provide small insights, but it is unlikely to provide you with meaningful information about your possible health risks.[37]

Please answer the following questions to reflect on some of the considerations discussed.

- Have you considered having your child take a DNA test?

- What are some of your concerns about testing DNA?

- Do you think your child should have input before they turn eighteen?

- Are you more likely to consider DNA testing in closed adoptions?

> NOTE It is very important to have an open discussion with your child before completing a DNA test, especially if there is the possibility that biological relatives may be found. Appropriate supervision is also critical with regards to reaching out to/communicating with DNA relatives.

LANGUAGE

When you adopt a child of color, particularly via international adoption, the child's birth culture often speaks a different language than the culture of your adoptive family. Some adoptive parents make efforts to learn and teach their adopted children about these things, but many do not.

Research has shown that internationally adopted children do not fit into the existing categories of bilingual language learning; the majority of children adopted internationally lose their bilingual status because their adoptive families are unable to maintain their birth language. What typically occurs is *arrested language development* in the adoptee—the premature stop of the growth of the child's birth language—as the adoptee develops their adopted language, which leaves the child at risk for failing to develop proficiency in either language.[38] Language loss is often observed in immigrants of all ages, but the speed of the loss in international adoptees is significant due to three factors:

1. Their low level of first language skills

2. Their lack of motivation for retaining their first language and their lack of opportunity to practice

3. Their lack of support for their first language in their adoptive family or community at large[39]

For example, Russian children who are adopted between the ages of four and eight often lose their native expressive language within three to six months of their adoption, and they typically lose all functional use of their birth language within a year of adoption. Infants and toddlers typically lose function of the birth language faster.[40] However, another study of Dutch adults who were adopted internationally from Korea found that children who were adopted between three to five months of age had a learning advantage from early exposure to a different language in their first half of life that left traces that may make it easier for them to relearn the language later on.[41]

Research has also found that many international adoptees have negative emotional reactions to hearing their birth language, which increases the risk of language loss over time.[42] Language has long since been identified as a powerful trigger for posttraumatic stress disorder, often because it is a representation of a person's life history. And adoptees, particularly older adoptees who have had traumatic pasts in orphanages or who have suffered abuse, can be triggered by their birth language. For other adoptees seeking to connect with their adoptive families and community, forgetting the language can have many immediate positive consequences by helping them blend in.[43]

> NOTE It is not unlikely for individuals to experience trauma responses to sensory input like hearing a language, especially if the initial traumatic experience occurred when the child was young. Infants and young children experience the world through their senses, which is why seeing/hearing/touching/smelling/tasting a certain sensation that correlates with early adverse experiences can be so activating.

When I started to dig into my identity as a Colombian adoptee, one of the biggest issues I had was not knowing the language of my birth culture. I had spent most of my life, up to that point, learning Italian, my adoptive father's language, from classes in school and interactions with family members. I had even learned some Portuguese in order to communicate with my grandmother on my adoptive mom's side. But I had not learned Spanish, the language I had heard for nine months in my birth mother's womb and for several months after in the orphanage. I knew less Spanish than most of my white friends, and I knew less than my adoptive parents.

Not knowing the language made me angry, resentful, and depressed. I hated that my parents, who knew Spanish, put their desires before what would have been best for me. They placed their culture and language in a place of higher importance in our family, even after I expressed a desire to learn Spanish.

- If your child's birth culture speaks a different language, has your family started to learn it? Are there classes in your area or online that teach that language?

- How can you save up to make this a priority in your family?

EXPLORING IDENTITY

Identity is difficult for most adoptees, but transracial adoptees have so many different aspects of it to consider. It took me years to become comfortable identifying as Latina. It took me even longer to become comfortable labeling myself as multiracial.

Claiming our identities as BIPOC is often difficult when we are raised by white parents in areas that aren't diverse. For *years* I was reluctant to claim my place as a woman of color because I felt *too* white. I didn't know how a Latina woman should act. I didn't think it was fair to claim that I was multiracial when I was literally raised to think I was a white woman. And eventually, when I was ready to claim that part of me, I did it without the support of my adoptive family. I was mocked for wanting to identify with my birth culture, for correcting family members when they referred to me as white. I also felt great shame for something that I felt should have come naturally.

I was also angry. Angry that the only experiences I had as a woman of color were negative. That when I was perceived as a POC was when I experienced microaggressions and racism from strangers. I yearned to know the joy of being a woman of color. I yearned to know the tastes of the food from my culture, to be familiar with music and traditions. And it was harder for me because my white adoptive parents didn't think it was important to expose me to this.

But the wonderful part of being an adult is that I can now explore my identity comfortably on my own. The years of slowly acclimating myself to Latinx culture have made me more comfortable in my own skin. They have made me love who I am, and now I can confidently talk about my identity.

BUT WHAT MAKES UP A PERSON'S IDENTITY?

When children start to grow up and come of age, they also typically begin to develop a strong sense of identity. From birth, a child's gender roles, history, relationships, and culture all help them form their own personal identity. During adolescence, teenagers' identity formation, decision-making, and coping strategies start to become independent from their parents, allowing for self-exploration.[44] Although we know that race is a social construct based on a person's physical characteristics, it is vital to acknowledge that people's biases toward people of color also have serious and often long-term ramifications.[45]

Having an ethnic identity is essential to developing self-identity in ethnic minorities. *Ethnic identification* is a process in which individuals learn to recognize their membership in racial groups and start to internalize particular traits associated with the group into their own self-identity. This concept focuses on the psychological implications of someone's commitment to their cultural heritage, allowing a person to feel close to thoughts, feelings, and actions that tend to be part of their own culture.[46]

Different stages are involved in developing a child's ethnic identity. During the first stage, *diffusion/foreclosure*, children begin to recognize race and ethnicity. The second stage, *moratorium*, is when early adolescents (around twelve years old) explore how they personally relate to their racial or ethnic group. The final stage, *achieved ethnic identity*, culminates with an individual understanding of culture-specific traditions, customs, and world view.[47]

NOTE Humans are naturally wired to sort/categorize. This can be by race, gender, other physical traits, etc. Kids as young as two or three will demonstrate this in their play.

Just in my day-to-day experience, I have found solid ground on which to stand to connect with biracial and multiracial individuals, like my husband, because they understand how it feels to struggle to fit into two or more different cultures. Poston's biracial identity development model helps me illustrate that biracial individuals experience conflict and periods of maladjustment while they are developing their identity. From my own experience, and from discussions I have had with other transracial adoptees, I have noticed how the biracial model can closely resemble similar experiences that we face as adoptees of color. Here are the five stages of Poston's biracial identity development model.[48]

Personal Identity: This stage occurs during childhood when the child is not aware of their mixed heritage.

Choice of Group Categorization: This stage occurs when the child is pressured to choose one racial category due to the influences of parents, peers, community, and society.

Enmeshment/Denial: In this stage, individuals feel disloyal and even guilty for choosing one racial identity over another.

Appreciation: In this stage, individuals explore other racial groups and can learn to appreciate them as well.

Integration: The person may identify more with one group and appreciates the integration of their multiple racial identities.

NOTE Loyalty binds are a common challenge adoptees face. They are placed in positions where it can feel like they must choose between biological and adoptive family, biological and adoptive race, biological and adoptive culture/traditions, and more.

It can be difficult to picture what these stages of identity mean for your children. When I was first introduced to the concept of identity development by my cross-cultural psychology teacher, I was honestly taken aback. It was surreal to see my experiences explained in such a black and white way that made me feel seen for one of the first times in my life. To help adoptive parents understand a little better, I have included some real-life examples from my experience.

─────────── **MELISSA'S IDENTITY DEVELOPMENT EXAMPLE:** ───────────

Personal Identity: I was unaware of my race and its importance until I was nineteen due to the secrecy of my adoption.

Choice of Group Categorization: After I found out I was adopted, I was overwhelmed and surrounded by white family, friends, and community, which made it difficult for me to identify as a multiracial Latina. At the time, it was easier to identify as Italian, like my adoptive parents.

Enmeshment/Denial: During this stage, I was in college, finally surrounded by a more diverse peer group that included a strong Latinx population. It was at this time that I felt the urge to learn more about my culture, but I ended up feeling too awkward and disloyal to my family to fully dig into my roots.

Appreciation: In college, I made concrete steps to work at learning more about my identity. I started listening to Latinx music and watching shows like *Jane the Virgin* that incorporated Latinx representation. Finally, I felt an appreciation for Latinx culture even though I wasn't fully immersed in it.

Integration: I am finally comfortable identifying as a multiracial Latina and am also comfortable with my cultural upbringing as Italian. I am successfully incorporating the Spanish language in my day-to-day life with my sons, and can appreciate and incorporate traditions from my adoptive parents' culture as well. To me, this looks like a diverse menu at Thanksgiving that includes empanadas and lasagna, or family parties where my grandparents speak to me in Italian while I play Reggaetón music.

When we are discussing identity development it is important to factor in the need for *Racial-ethnic socialization*. This is the process of socializing children within their own race or ethnicity, encouraging racial-ethnic pride, and teaching children of color how to cope with racism, discrimination, and racial oppression. Parents who do not practice this may not have received education about racial-ethnic socialization, its importance, and how to implement it in a healthy way.

JANET E. HELMS'S MODEL FOR WHITE RACIAL DEVELOPMENT

I feel that it is also essential to discuss Janet E. Helms's model for *white racial development* due to the impact that white adoptive parents have on their adopted children of color. If white parents are unable to embrace their own racial identity, how can they teach their children the importance of embracing their ethnic identity?

Contact: Obliviousness to one's whiteness and the implications of racial-group differences. Generally, this stage means you adhere to a colorblind mentality.

Disintegration: Confusion and guilt are at the forefront because you have become consciously aware of your membership and identity as a white person and the moral dilemmas that come with it.

Reintegration: Your blame-the-victim attitude is dominant, and even when you admit that white privilege exists, you may feel that it is because people of color deserve it.

Pseudo-independence: Generally, in this stage you do not feel that whites deserve privileges, but you still look to people of color to confront racism rather than being actively nonracist yourself.

Immersion/Emersion: You make an effort to develop a meaningful and moral definition of whiteness and connecting to your own white identity while also working toward being actively anti-racist.

Autonomy: You reach this last stage when you are finally able to have a positive racial identity with your whiteness as well as actively pursue social justice.

ACTIVITY:
ADOPTIVE PARENT IDENTITY DEVELOPMENT

For white adoptive parents, it can be difficult to understand the importance of race in their transracially adopted children's lives until they understand their own racial identity. This is why I am urging you to really consider each stage of Helms's model and ask yourselves these questions:

1. Where do I currently fit into Helms's white racial development model?

2. Where do I want to be? And why?

3. What are five concrete steps I can take to get there?

4. What are some challenges I am apt to face on the way? What can I do to make getting where I want to be easier?

Once you are able to discuss these questions openly and honestly, I believe you can better understand and empathize with your children of color. Understanding your own racial identity is a difficult process on its own, but raising children of another race and teaching them how to understand their own identities adds another complex layer. You can manage it, however, if you are willing to do the work and ask for guidance from your child's Latinx, Black, Indigenous community that you have worked to create a relationship with.

NOTE *Inside Transracial Adoption* by Beth Hall and Gail Steinberg and *Me and White Supremacy* by Layla Saad are great resources to dive deeper.

ACTIVITY:
GRADE YOUR COMMUNITY

While your home may seem like it is in the perfect community that is safe and has access to the "best" schools, it may not be as perfect as it seems. Often many white adoptive parents live in neighborhoods that are also primarily white, which means that there is typically a lack of diversity and inclusion.

Please grade your community from A–F in the following categories.

- Diversity

    _____ The school makeup of your public/private school is diverse.

    _____ Public spaces are representative of the people in the community.

- Bias

    _____ The community is dedicated to anti-racism.

    _____ There are programs in place to address racism and discrimination.

- Race-Based Crime

    _____ BIPOC people are safe in the community in which you live.

- White Saviorism

    _____ Community members feel the need to rescue BIPOC.

- Social Supports

    _____ The community invests in childcare, affordable medical care, and similar supports for every child.

LEVEL UP If your child is older, have them grade the community/environments they are commonly in and see how the grades line up with yours.

CHAPTER 3 REFLECTION QUESTIONS

- Where do you currently fit into Helms's white racial development model? Where do you want to be? And why?

- What are five concrete steps you can take to get there?

- What are some challenges you will face on the way? What can you do to make getting where you want to be easier?

- In order to help your child develop a healthy identity as a person of color, what can you do?

- What are some other examples of inequalities influenced by centering whiteness that can impact your child of color?

- How old were you when you first realized people had different skin colors?

- Can you look back at your childhood and share racist events that you now see for what they were? Example: In high school the theatre club had white teens spray tan to a much darker skin tone so they would appear Latino for their parts in *West Side Story*.

- How has your opinion of situations like the one in the previous example changed as you've become more aware of racism?

- How old was your BIPOC child when they started to become curious about physical and cultural differences? How old were they when they talked about having a different skin tone than you and/or your partner?

- How can you incorporate your child's birth culture or language consistently?

- In what ways can your family connect and make authentic relationships with your child's BIPOC community?

TIPS TO REMEMBER

1. Children often learn by modeling, so it is essential that you model the conversations you want your children to have in order for them to explore their identities.

2. Embrace what being a white person means in our society and engage in conversations about your culture and the privileges it may grant you.

3. If you aren't ready to give it your all, practice these conversations with a partner before engaging in them with your kids. It is important to refrain from blaming or guilting one another and use these discussions to explore and validate everyone's experiences.

4

TRAUMA AND ADOPTION

According to the American Psychological Association, *trauma* is an emotional response to a terrible event like an accident or natural disaster that can cause flashbacks, physical symptoms (headaches, stomachaches, etc.), and unpredictable emotions. Whenever you think about adoption, it is important to note that due to maternal separation, your child will have some type of trauma to cope with throughout their life. From the moment I became pregnant, doctors, family, and books all reminded me of how important it was to take care of myself because my baby could feel everything. From my stress, to the food I ate, to the music I listened to—it all affected my child for better or for worse. But something seems to happen to make people forget the importance of these influences when the pregnant person is considering adoption, and that same something often puts adoptive parents on a pedestal.

In this chapter we will be discussing the cycle of grief in adoption, maternal separation, toxic positivity, and mental health.

TRAUMA IN ADOPTION

When children are adopted, at any age, they experience the trauma of being separated from their birth family. But what about when they are adopted as infants? Is there trauma then?

In infancy and early childhood, children attach and bond with their primary caregiver; this bond can be influenced by gestation, their mother's health, and genetic vulnerabilities.[1] Mothers can differentiate their infant's smell from another baby, and babies show a strong preference for clothes worn by their moms.[2] Newborns also show a preference for their mothers compared to other caregivers, even while they are still in the womb.[3] So yes, even a newborn child can experience trauma and grief when separated from their birth mother.[4] The grief that adopted children feel is real and should be validated because it affects them their whole lives. Children who have experienced trauma or neglect experience further complications, but all adopted children grieve the loss of their biological family, heritage, and culture to some degree.[5]

Studies have found that any type of separation from parents, as the result of anything from trauma to military deployment, is very stressful for children. Such separation can lead to anxiety and acting out, even if the child has the support of family and communities. When a caregiver isn't present, children undergo long-term stress that can lead to genetic changes and abnormal physiological functioning.[6] Not only are adoptees four times more likely to attempt suicide, but studies have also shown that they experience problems with mental illnesses at a higher rate than nonadopted persons.[7]

> NOTE Research tells us that separating an infant from their mother is like their death to the child. The emotional pain of this separation impacts the same parts of the brain that are impacted by intense physical pain.

The idea that children who are adopted by loving families are better off and do not experience trauma from being separated from their biological family is deeply problematic to me as an adoptee, especially since nurses and doctors repeatedly emphasized the importance of bonding and genetic history while I was pregnant.

One of the first things that I learned when I was pregnant was about the importance of skin-to-skin contact immediately after birth. Newborn babies are placed on their mother's chest, skin to skin typically, between the mother's breasts, dressed only in a diaper, so the front of the baby's body is in direct contact with the mother's skin. This provides the infant with warmth and stimulation. Preterm newborns who have skin-to-skin contact have been found to have more stable heart rates, temperatures, and respiratory rates. Some studies show that babies at twelve months old who received skin-to-skin contact at birth are likely to perform better on development scales as well. Mothers who have this experience also report more positive maternal feelings, less depression, and more empowerment in their role as parents because the feel-good hormone, oxytocin, is released during this first contact.[8]

It simply baffles me that, when it comes to adoption, these formative postpartum moments are almost pushed aside to focus on the infallible positive adoption narrative. The idea that separating a child from their first family at birth or any time after is a perfect solution without consequences is a disservice to the child, the adoptive family, and the birth family. Adoptive parents need to recognize that even a newborn can experience difficulties from being separated from their mother. If they don't acknowledge the trauma, adoptive parents cannot make informed decisions to help their child develop properly or cope with the stress that trauma can cause.

TRAUMA-INFORMED PARENTING

When you adopt a child, it is important that you become prepared to embrace trauma-informed parenting in your family. According to the University of Buffalo Center for Social Research, "Trauma-Informed Care understands and considers the pervasive nature of trauma and promotes environments of healing and recovery rather than practices and services that may inadvertently re-traumatize."[9]

Trauma-Informed Parenting Tips

Here are some things parents/guardians can do to help:

TAKE TIME TO UNDERSTAND THE REPERCUSSIONS OF THE CHILD'S TRAUMA. Connect with your child and dedicate time to open lines of communication so you can understand their behaviors and personalities. Each child is unique, and what may work for one child may not work for another. Weekly family check-ins over breakfast can be a great way to communicate about schedules, emotional well-being, responsibilities, and family activities.[10]

PROVIDE A COMFORTABLE ENVIRONMENT IN WHICH YOUR CHILD CAN FEEL SAFE. Reinforce schedules and discuss ways to keep your child safe at home and in school. Although safety may seem obvious, it can be more complex for children who have experienced trauma. This may make it necessary for you to find different ways to reassure your child. For example, parents can also support children's feeling of safety by providing snacks that they can keep in their rooms or verbal reinforcement. For children who have experienced food insecurity, it can be helpful to reinforce that they no longer need to worry about where their next meal will come from. When a child has grown up and experienced hunger, it can take a while for them to lose habits that helped them survive. It's also important to remember that a safe home also means adoptive parents should become safe listeners with whom children can discuss abuse and trauma in their pasts. Encourage your child to work through distorted beliefs and provide ways to preserve memories.

HELP YOUR CHILD LABEL THEIR EMOTIONS AND ENCOURAGE SAFE COPING MECHANISMS. Some children who experience trauma can have a difficult time figuring out more nuanced emotions because of the fear, frustration, and sometimes anger that they are so used to having to cope with. Model identifying emotions in your day-to-day life and practice with your child until it becomes a habit. Modeling this behavior can help children learn how to explain difficult feelings and why they may act out, and in turn, it can help you create healthier coping mechanisms as a preventative.

PRACTICE SELF-CARE. Trauma-informed parenting is very important, but it can be so easy for parents/guardians to get overwhelmed when they are interacting with people who have such strong emotions and complex histories. It is imperative for parents to take care of their own mental and physical health so they can remain patient, kind, and understanding.

ACTiViTY:
PARENTiNG STRATEGiES

As humans, we learn a lot through what we see others do, and because of this, a lot of us will have some parenting habits that were passed down from our mothers and fathers. Some of those strategies can be very effective, but when we are thinking about parenting an adoptive or foster child in particular, we need to consider the resiliency of the child and the impact trauma can have on them. For this exercise, please start by taking a moment to write down what type of parenting your parents or guardians used with you and your siblings growing up.

Next, answer the following questions:

- Did your parents ever parent you in a way that hurt you?

- How did your parents react when angry?

- How do you manage your anger or frustration?

- How do you manage disagreements with your spouse or partner, and how do you think that would impact a child who would be exposed to that in their day-to-day lives?

- Have you ever addressed childhood events that hurt you?

- How is your relationship with your parents?

- Would you parent your child the same way your parents did? Why or why not?

- What are some more gentle parenting methods that you can use with an adoptive or foster child?

ADOPTION AND PRIVILEGE

There's this idea (that even fellow adoptees have) that adopting a child of color and providing a loving and nurturing home makes adoptive parents immune to being racist. Maybe in an ideal world that would be true, but unfortunately, this is not an ideal world. Adopting a child of color does not mean that you aren't racist, just like having a best friend who is a BIPOC doesn't mean you're not racist.

Recently I was reminded of this idea by a fellow international adoptee who told me that he "never realized how much hate there is from adopted children of color who have white parents." He went on to deny that my parents, and other white adoptive parents, could possibly be racist toward their adoptive children of color. This, admittedly, hurt since it came from another adoptee who was basically dismissing my lived experiences of racism within my own family, along with the experiences of many other adoptees. This message was a vivid reminder that not all adoptees have the same experience. Because the positive narrative of adoption is so prevalent, another adoptee found it difficult to believe my adoptive parents could be racist.

The article posted on *Medium* by Melea VanOstrand, titled "'I'm Not Racist. I Have a Black Family Member!' I'm That Black Family Member, and Yes, You Are Racist," includes many gems, but one line stood out to me. It described the response Melea had to her sister saying that she didn't see her as Black, that she was simply her sister. VanOstrand said, "And she's right. That's who I am to her. Not her Black sister. But, to the rest of the world, I am a Black woman. They aren't color-blind like she is."[11] VanOstrand eloquently stated in a few lines what I had been trying to get my family to understand for years. That despite my being "one of them," as my mom so often says, others don't view me or treat me as white, and in turn, I am not protected by their whiteness as an adult. The world views me as a Latina woman and treats me like one. They make assumptions about me that many people make about other Latina women: they assume that I speak broken English, clean homes for a living, or am otherwise "less than."

Despite a "love is love" or "love is enough" dominant narrative in adoption, many adopted children of color struggle with their identities, and white parents who cling to this narrative are doing their children a disservice. Love will be enough for many families until it's not, and what is important for adoptive parents to realize is that their privilege will not protect their children of color indefinitely. A time comes when all children of color face discrimination and racism, whether by strangers, friends, or family. This is why white adoptive parents need to be willing to do the work and learn how to prepare children for a world that does see color. Acknowledging the privilege of being a white adoptive parent will help you bridge the gap within your adoptive family and embrace being a multicultural family.

NOTE When it comes to trauma, especially when it comes to helping clients and families understand the nuances of the various types of trauma associated with adoption, I commonly talk about making space for both/and instead of forcing an either/or. What I mean by this is that adoption is complex; there is *both* grief *and* joy, *both* loss *and* gain, and there needs to be space for both. Taking a stance that says there has to be one or the other, either/or, can inevitably invalidate or deny an individual's experience.

ACTiViTY:
COMMENT QUALiTY CONTROL

The following is a list of a few different articles written by adoptees or featuring adoptees. Go to each and write down a positive and negative comment from each.

- "I was a foster child. Foster care adoptions won't solve the end of Roe," by Andrew Bridge, www.washingtonpost.com/opinions/2022/08/10/foster-care-adoptions-roe-abortion/

- "I Was Adopted. I Know the Trauma It Can Inflict," by Elizabeth Spiers, www.nytimes.com/2021/12/03/opinion/adoption-supreme-court-amy-coney-barrett.html

- "What a Black Woman Wishes Her Adoptive White Parents Knew," by Mariama J. Lockington, www.buzzfeednews.com/article/mariamalockington/what-a-black-woman-wishes-her-adoptive-white-parents-knew

Go to a few of the following adoptees' Instagram or TikTok accounts, look at their most popular posts, and write down a positive and negative comment from each.

ADOPTEE INSTAGRAM PAGES

- @adoptee_thoughts by Melissa Guida-Richards

- @anne_heffron by Anne Heffron

- @fereraswan by Ferera Swan

- @hannahjacksonmatthews by Hannah Matthews

- @patrickintheworld by Patrick Armstrong

- @therapyredeemed by Cam Lee Small, MS (*Adoption-informed therapist*)

- @thisadopteelife by Amanda

- @wreckageandwonder by Torie DiMartile

ADOPTEE TIKTOK PAGES

- https://www.tiktok.com/@miathaicha

- https://www.tiktok.com/@karpoozy

- https://www.tiktok.com/@thewardofthestate2.0

- https://www.tiktok.com/@pittiemama87

- https://www.tiktok.com/@wildheartcollective

- https://www.tiktok.com/@taylorruipingshen

- https://www.tiktok.com/@intersectionaladoptee

Do you see a trend? How do you think negative comments like these affect the adopted person?

What can you do to support adoptees?

How would you feel if your child was sharing their experiences and received some of the negative comments you saw were left for adoptees and former foster youth?

NOTE The reality is that we can all become reactive in certain situations, especially in the age of technology. The problem is that being reactive often has fallout to some degree. This is why it is so important that, whether we are in social media spaces or in face-to-face interactions, we learn to practice responding instead of reacting. *Reacting* is instant, impulsive, occurs without much thought, and is often at an unconscious level. *Responding*, on the other hand, is a much slower process; it involves more awareness. You are able to identify and acknowledge your thoughts/emotions and mindfully choose a course of action.

REUNION

My adoptive father and grandmother passed away within a few months of one another. The pain of these monumental losses has come in waves ever since. But what I find interesting is that in the same year, I reconnected with my birth mother, and I feel the same loss and pain for the relationship with the woman who gave me life. I feel loss for the family I will never quite feel like I belong with. And I feel anger and frustration that I cannot even communicate with my *family* without an app that translates Spanish for me. As I painstakingly double and triple check the messages I send, I worry that I may scare them away. And I worry about their safety in the midst of a pandemic that prevents me from meeting them.

On top of it all, I feel guilty for being interested in my birth family as my mother and I grieve my father. And if you're wondering why I'm sharing this, it's because these things are often not talked about. Many adoptees are unaware of the actual ins and outs involved in reunion because the media/adoptive parents/agencies dominate the narrative. Even if you are aware of the complexities of reunion, nothing really prepares you for feeling like an outsider from your biological relatives. From your own mother.

I found my birth mother almost a year ago and have yet to find the courage to try to speak to her without the buffer of someone translating. I fear disappointing her and am ashamed that I am not able to even talk to her myself. So, when you talk about how adoption is beautiful, please make space for adoptees to share the nuances to help them spread the truth of the pain that is also a very real part of adoption. We *need* to make space for these complex feelings and experiences as well.

ACTiViTY:
HOLiDAYS TO REMEMBER

Please make space for your adopted child during this holiday season. Create traditions to help them connect with their birth family. Hug them if they need to cry, and make sure they have a healthy way to express their emotions. Holidays are supposed to be a time when family can be together.

When you're an adoptee, seeing the joy of families being together can be extremely painful. Discussions you hear about family trees, traits that have been passed down, or even family photos can be a trigger. One of the most awkward, even painful, things about the holidays for adoptees of color is being the only BIPOC in the room.

A simple, yet effective, activity to help your adopted child during these special days is to make space for them emotionally and physically. Here are some quick-and-easy ways to make sure your child's birth family is included during special occasions.

- Set a spot at the dinner table for a birth mother or father as a visual reminder for your child so that they know their birth parent(s) is loved and cherished in your family.

- Set aside wall space for pictures, letters, or mementos that remind your child of their birth family.

- Create a special playlist of traditional music from your child's birth culture.

- Schedule an extra therapy session for your child during the holiday week.

- Plan for an extra hour or two of downtime so your house is quiet and your child has a safe place in which to unwind and simply feel what they need to feel.

- Utilize sensory tools like the Harkla Hug's Sensory Pea Pod, a sensory swing, a weighted blanket, or a sensory sack to help encourage your child's self-regulation.

These activities/actions are a great starting point from which you can make space for your child's birth family. In addition, taking steps like this can help guide your child to develop healthy coping mechanisms they can use to work through the complex emotions brought up during the holidays.

NOTE Quite often adopted children experience a build-up in dysregulation around holiday times. Children's dysregulation can start a couple weeks prior, peak on or around the holiday, and may take another few days or even weeks to get back down to a baseline.

MISSING HISTORY

I was going through some documents from my adoption and found my first Colombian passport and a picture of me at a few months that I'd never seen before. It's a small thing, and it's something that many people don't understand the privilege of.

Seeing this picture of myself as a baby makes me want to cry for the child who did not have a mother to love on and care for her in the first pivotal months of her life. The child didn't have a baby book or a stash of a million pictures of baby hair and tiny toes. I wasn't able to grieve this loss until now because it wasn't until recently that I even realized other families had pictures of their moms pregnant or postpartum holding the baby. My life seemed to have started the moment I entered the US, but now I'm discovering the ties that were broken and left behind.

ACTIVITY:
PREPPING FOR QUESTIONS ABOUT FAMILY HISTORY

One way I was able to find some peace with my missing family history and the five months I spent in the orphanage was by writing down all the questions to which I wanted answers. You can adapt this activity for a child of any age who has questions about their missing past. It can be very empowering for us to just put the words out there instead of having them weigh us down throughout our day-to-day lives.

Encourage your child to start compiling questions they have for their birth parent, adoption social worker, the foster parent they had once, or anyone else who is no longer in their lives. Questions can be as simple as "What color are your eyes?" or more complex, like "Why did you place me for adoption?" No question is too silly or too personal in this activity. What is important is that your child has the freedom and support to feel safe enough to ask these questions in a controlled environment.

I suggest purchasing a question box specifically for this purpose or have your child use a journal dedicated to this activity. No matter what, there is no wrong way to do this activity.

It is important for you to encourage your child to engage in this activity while also respecting their privacy. Do not pressure your child to share the letters and questions with you. This activity is aimed at making your child feel safe enough to express curiosity, love, and even anger toward their birth parents and providing them with a safe place to do so.

> LEVEL UP Have your child/teen write a letter or draw a picture from the perspective of certain parts of themselves. That is, the part of them that is angry about having limited information, the part of them that is sad about not being able to have contact with their biological family, the part that is confused about why they don't have baby pictures like their peers, and so on.

THE CYCLE OF GRIEF

Once I started to publicly discuss my story, I learned quickly that other adoptive parents and relatives typically met me with the same resistance that I'd encountered from my parents. My viral post "My Adoptive Parents Hid My Racial Identity for 19 Years" led to dozens of emails and comments from angry adoptive parents and others who felt like adoption was a miracle I should be grateful for.[12]

I received an email from an anonymous reader on April 5, 2019; in it they said:

> *I just read your article in the Huffington Post and am horrified and sad. You are a human being, the only race of humans on the planet. I cannot begin to say how offensive and hurtful your words are and how racist they come across.*

Another equally angry person wrote to me on April 12, 2019.

> *You have no Colombian culture—you're an American. You have American culture—or at least you should. "Your people" go by the titles of "mom" and "dad." Your rejection of them shows a colossal lack of maturity. Grow up, or do us all a favor and move back to Columbia.*

Most of the angry emails came from those who believed that I was lucky to have been adopted and that I didn't have the right to criticize my parents despite the trauma their actions caused. What I found most interesting was the overwhelming responsibility others felt to protect or fight to protect my parents' reputation. This need seemed to stem from the discord between my account and the dominant positive adoption narrative. What these people didn't know is that I had discussed sharing my story with my parents and had their support. I wonder . . . if they knew my parents supported me, would they be so angry? Would they tell me to go back to the same country they just claimed I had no ties with?

The problem with this anger is that it wasn't just aimed at me or my story. Almost every conversation, video, or blog post I read by other adoptees that discussed the difficulties they face was met with anger, denial, and bargaining by adoptive parents on the internet.

In 2018, Steve J. made a Facebook comment to Nicole Chung's essay, "People Want to Hear That I'm Happy I Was Adopted. It's Not That Simple." He said that "I hope no one decides against international adoption based on this lady's experience. It is atypical and probably the result of isolation in a small, remote, homogenous community."[13]

It seemed to me that any efforts to diversify the adoption narrative, especially by adoptees who were personally affected by adoption, were immediately met with aggressive, angry, or fearful responses to shut them down. When I saw these types of comments repeatedly, it made me realize that many white adoptive parents seem to experience a *cycle of grief* when they learn about the challenges adoptive children have faced and the injustices in the adoption system. Some people refer to this as adoptive parents coming out of their own fog. More specifically, I think of this as a process that adoptive parents need to work through to become truly aware of the problems caused by the white savior mentality.

I believe that parents have to fully mourn the ideal adoption to be able to truly sympathize and empathize with their adoptees who are coming out of the fog. If they don't, the conversation and understanding between adoptive parents, birth moms, and adoptees cannot be as honest and meaningful as it needs to be to help the adoption community move in the right direction. When they learn more about the full scope of birth moms' and adoptees' adoption experiences and more of the nuanced history, adoptive parents can become overwhelmed; that is when the first stage of grief immediately kicks in.

Let's take a closer look at each stage of the cycle parents go through.

NOTE Keep in mind that the grief cycle is different for each person, does not have a definitive ending, and is not linear in nature. An individual may grieve differently based on their developmental level and may return to certain stages as they age.

Denial

When many adoptive parents are first faced with the idea that their child's life has had complications, they often instinctually deny it. It is natural to get defensive about a concept that we have held near and dear to our hearts for many years. White adoptive parents in this situation are confronted with the reality that they could not protect their child from the pain of racism, isolation, and/or trauma. They also have to face the reality that they might have caused harm, which might be even more painful.

Ignoring another person's pain is easy as long as you keep looking in different directions, surround yourself with only people who agree with you, and simply quiet down or cancel the offender. It's easy to say "not all adoptees feel that way" when you are the person holding power in the dynamic.

NOTE Disenfranchised grief and ambiguous loss are two very important terms to be aware of when it comes to adoptees and birth families. Disenfranchised grief speaks to the fact that losses associated with adoption are not acknowledged societally; there are no formal mourning rituals for these losses as there are for other losses people experience. This lack of acknowledgment actually prolongs emotional pain. Ambiguous loss is characterized as a loss that likely will not lead to any point of emotional closure or clear understanding for the individual.

As an adoptive parent, it can be hard to get open and honest feedback when adoptees and birth mothers are either afraid or too nervous to share their actual feelings. The problem is that by refusing to listen or being in denial, adoptive parents are only making the situation worse for the adoptee in the long run.

Some of the defensive comments I received from adoptive parents responding to an essay I published, titled "Abby Johnson's Video Shows the Problem with White Parents Adopting Children of Color," show these dynamics. This article discussed the Republican National Convention 2020 speaker Abby Johnson's remarks about how it was smart for police officers to profile her Black (adopted) son but not her white sons.[14] Here is one of the comments on the post that illustrate this defensiveness:

> *Though I agree, as an adoptive parent, with much of this story, it fails to address one glaring issue. For a significant number of these children, a white adoptive home may not be the ideal placement. It is, however, the only permanent placement available to them. Whatever inadequacies the adoptive parents might have in dealing with race, "color blindness," and other issues—it is impossible to accept that these children would have been better off left to be raised in and by a broken system. Children, all children, deserve to grow up in a home where they are wanted and belong.*[15]

My response to comments like these is to say that thinking that adoption is a simple either/or situation is not helpful to anyone in the adoption triad. Yes, many children need homes, but it is often because the system does not support their birth families and because flaws in the system are often ignored. After all, adoption agencies do not make their profit by helping to preserve families; they profit off of adoptions by mainly white adoptive parents.

Anger

Once denial takes hold, adoptive parents often shift from ignoring the problem to becoming angry at people who are trying to ruin the perfect picture of adoption that they cherished. They may argue with their adoptive children when the adoptees discuss challenges they faced, they may lash out at adoptees and birth mothers who tell their stories in the media or online, and they may simply be aggressive toward anyone expressing an opposing viewpoint.

Anger might also crop up when adoptive parents complete the cycle of grief and swing back to the beginning stages and aim their anger toward adult adoptees, fellow adoptive parents, adoption agencies, and themselves. This can be dangerous because it can lead to a sense of hopelessness that also does not support the adoptee. Adoptive parents act this out in angry messages to transracial adoptees calling them ungrateful and in public Facebook threads arguing against adoptees' lived experiences; they even publicly shame adoption practices as being unethical processes without taking responsibility for their part in them.

Once adoptive parents become aware of the ethical issues within adoption and the lack of support for birth parents, adult adoptees, and even adoptive parents, it can be easy for some parents to become keyboard warriors toward other adoptive parents online. This shows up as snippy and even angry comments about adoption practices in adoption groups on Facebook, or as them expressing outrage about certain things, but providing little to no follow-through to support actual change.

Bargaining

Once adoptive parents are exposed to enough conversations about the nuances of adoption, they might open up to admit that problems do occur. This usually means adoptive parents are willing to accept some of the information and that they may even agree that there are more systemic issues that they do not feel individually responsible for. I've found that many adoptive parents openly admit that there are problems such as child trafficking and a lack of support for adoptees and birth parents, but they have a harder time accepting the more controversial issues.

In this stage of grief, adoptive parents openly try to discuss topics they deem acceptable but cling to phrases like "not all adoptive parents," "not all adoptees feel that way," or "but I know an adoptee who is happy even though _____ and _____ happens sometimes." They often stick to the "love is enough" narrative and ignore the problems that racism and white saviors can cause. However, once they work through these feelings, they often become distraught and overwhelmed as their eyes open to the other side of adoption.

Depression

In my experience talking with adoptive parents, this stage is often the most overwhelming and confusing. I can see them try to understand systemic issues while struggling with their belief in an infallible adoption system. But not being able to have something that they realize is an unattainable perfection portrayed by the media, friends, adoption agencies, and so on is depressing. Adoptive parents really struggle to learn a way to contribute to bettering the adoption system. It can become exhausting and isolating to embrace this controversial new narrative, especially when your fellow adoptive parents are no longer on the same page.

In adoptive communities, some of the questions often heard are, "How can I prevent my child from experiencing trauma?" or "So my child will always be hurt by adoption?" There are no clear-cut answers to such questions at this time, though some may advocate for adoptions to be eliminated or for white parents not to adopt transracially. Personally, I am not anti-adoption, but I am for family preservation first. It took me a while to come to this opinion because, at first, I was really angry at the adoption industry. When I was adopted, no protections were in place to make sure my parents got enough education, and no one followed through to make sure my parents told me I was adopted. But after a lot of research and after numerous conversations with everyone in the adoption community, I firmly believe that adoption needs to be an option.

I also strongly believe that not enough effort is being made to keep families together when a little financial and educational support could help make that possible. However, in some situations, adoption is still the safest option for the child. The adoption industry and community does need to acknowledge, however, that currently, not enough is being done to make sure adoptive parents receive continued education and counseling in transracial adoption to help support them as their child ages. There is some focus on introductory information like haircare and navigating the adoption system, but little information is provided about identity formation, cultural immersion, and anti-racist work; this type of information needs to be prioritized.

The reality is that about 70 percent of adoptive parents are white, so the likelihood of transracial adoptions occurring is high. It can be difficult to hear all the controversial opinions that go against the very nature of white adoptive parents thinking adoption is the perfect solution. Only when you are ready to fully accept that it isn't black and white can you move on to the next stage.

Acceptance

In my opinion, this stage is almost unattainable. To attain it, adoptive parents need to find an equilibrium where they can absorb their newfound knowledge without reacting negatively or centering themselves in apologies and commentary. This includes accepting that some parts of the system are almost impossible to change or that it will take dozens of years to make the kind of progress that those of us out of the fog want to see.

Some adoptive parents can achieve some semblance of acceptance if they work hard, but in my experience, this is often a slippery slope. As is the case for adoptees experiencing grief, the cycle of grief can often mean that adoptive parents switch back and forth between the stages. It is just a part of life. It is human instinct to protect ourselves from pain, and admitting that there are problems that you cannot fix is difficult. This is why I've only ever seen one or two adoptive parents stay in this stage for long.

ACTiViTY:
CYCLE OF GRiEF

After taking a look at the cycle of grief we just discussed, consider where you fit in each of the categories. Have you had experience with each? With a few? Elaborate in a notebook or on a separate piece of paper.

LEVEL UP On your own or with your child, reflect on what kind of mourning rituals would be appropriate for this kind of grief/loss.

THE DICHOTOMY OF A BIRTH PARENT

Although this chapter allows us to see the different ways adoptees are viewed, we also need to look at how family members and society view birth parents. On the one hand, by some, birth parents are seen as selfless people who are making a family's dream come true, and on the other, they are seen as awful people for throwing away their child.

Adoptive parents also need to understand the complexity of how everyone perceives birth parents and how this impacts their adopted child. For instance, an adopted child may find Mother's Day complicated because they want to celebrate their birth mother/parent too, or they may want to know who their birth mother/parent is. Many of us are often told that we were given up because our birth parent loved us so much, but at some point in our lives, we also can hear terrible things about the choices our birth parent made in our lives. The negative perception that pigeon-holes birth parents often complicates the way we look at them, and this often leads to more misconceptions.

> NOTE Even if limited information is known about a child's biological father, it is important for adoptive parents to acknowledge that the child does have a biological father. Often a great amount of focus is placed on the biological mother, which can leave kids confused, feeling left out, or different.

Take a few moments to brainstorm about your perceptions of birth parents and write your responses in the space provided:

Describe positive characteristics of birth parents.

Describe negative characteristics of birth parents.

Just like any person, birth parents are neither completely good nor evil. They are humans, just trying to do their best. Some birth parents have experienced terrible trauma and abuse in their lives, some had easy childhoods, some are disabled, and others struggle with drug or alcohol addiction. Like everyone else in the world, there is no one type of birth parent. It is toxic to make assumptions about someone based on a choice they made during a difficult time in their lives.

ACTIVITY:
CARTOON MIRRORS

I have the pleasure of including a two-page comic strip by the artist Joe Seurg, who is also a birth father. Joe created this after he saw a picture of his son and noticed how much darker he was compared to his classmates in school. It made him think about his own struggles growing up multiracial.

For this activity, read the accompanying comic and answer the following questions:

- Have you ever considered how birth fathers feel about adoption?

- What ways do you think adoptive parents can support children and birth parents when sharing photos/mementos in open adoptions?

- How did you feel after reading the comic strip?

- Throughout your life, have there been any moments in which you felt like you didn't fit in?

- How do you think the artist viewed the term *hapa* versus how others saw it?

For context, the term *hapa*, the Hawaiian word for "part," is commonly used by multiracial Asian-Americans. It is important to know that some people do argue that it is a slur and compare it to words like *half-breed* or *mulatto*. But according to Kealalōkahi Losch, a professor of Hawaiian studies, its original use was not derogatory. Some Asian Americans or Hawaiian people prefer to use the term and some do not; it is a personal decision that others should respect.

WHAT'S HAPANING

ARTIST: JOE SEURG, BIRTH FATHER

ACTIVITY:
BIRTH PARENTS CONSULT

For this activity, I am encouraging adoptive parents to get to know birth parents, and not just the ones you are looking to match with for a placement. Seek out a birth parent consultation with a person who placed their child for adoption. Make sure you compensate them for their time and please respect their boundaries.

Here are some potential questions you might ask:

- How do you feel the adoptive parents could have supported you better?

- What did the adoptive parents do that you *did* feel was helpful?

- If you have experience with open adoption, do you feel comfortable sharing what you like/don't like about it?

- How could you have been more supported at the birth?

- Did you receive post-adoption supports from the agency?

- How do you feel about adoption advertising by prospective adoptive parents?

- How do you feel about adoption fundraisers?

Add your questions here:

LEVEL UP Before asking lots of questions, simply open the floor for birth parents to share their experience with you. Let them know you are there to listen and learn, not to judge. Challenge yourself to just listen to their experience and note what stands out without even having to ask a specific question. Resist urges to cut them off, shut down, react with defensiveness, or give in to anger if there are responses you do not agree with.

Please review some of the resources below to learn more about birth mothers' perspectives.

RESOURCES ABOUT BIRTH MOTHERS

- Ashley Mitchell, "Ask Ashley: Dear Prospective Adoptive Parent," www .bigtoughgirl.com/askashley

- Melissa Guida-Richards, "Birth Mothers Share What They Want Adoptive Parents to Know," https://theeverymom.com/what-birth-mothers-want -adoptive-parents-to-know/

- "Birth Mothers Amplified," www.youtube.com/channel/UCjQiuquTCt6 Wi4pR7xuWrVw

CHAPTER 4 REFLECTION QUESTIONS

- Have you discussed adoption trauma with friends and family?

- How will you protect your child's story?

- How can you advocate for your child in school with assignments like family trees?

- Does adoption trauma make you nervous about adopting?

- If you were in crisis, unhoused, pregnant, with only a few dollars to your name, and without the friends/family/connections you have now, how would you get back on your feet?

- Has your view of birth parents changed over time?

- Have you ever spoken or listened to birth parent stories?

- What misconceptions have you had about birth parents?

- What ways can you support birth parents in your community?

- Does the adoption agency you are considering support family preservation?

- If you are adopting through private adoption, will you provide funds for healthcare/housing/and the like for expectant parents? Will you expect the money back if the pregnant person decides not to choose adoption?

- How would it make you feel if an expectant parent chose to parent?

- Will you use adoption ads? Why or why not?

- How can you support your child's connection with their birth family?

5

MENTAL HEALTH AND THERAPY

Whether you are an adoptive parent, an adoptee, or a birth parent, it is vital that you deal with past trauma and prioritize your mental health. But what is mental health? Mental health includes your psychological, social, and emotional well-being. Well-managed mental health can help you lower your risk of illness, manage your stress, and even increase your energy levels.[1]

Adverse Childhood Experiences (ACEs) are potentially traumatic events that occur between birth and seventeen. Some ACEs are obvious, such as neglect, physical or mental abuse, or even the death of a family member. However, many people do not realize that this includes losing a parent through separation, divorce, or, yes—adoption. By the time a child is placed in a foster or adoptive home, they are very likely to have experienced multiple ACEs, which can lead to depression, chronic diseases, social problems, or even financial difficulties.[2]

ACEs can have detrimental consequences that affect a person's well-being long term and can make adoptees or foster youth more likely to become involved in sex trafficking, teen pregnancy, and have an increased risk of suicide. Research shows that the more ACEs a child has, the more likely it is that they will have difficulty maintaining or forming healthy relationships and the more likely they are to experience complications from ongoing stress that are only exacerbated by systemic racism or even poverty.[3]

SUPPORTING THE MENTAL HEALTH OF FOSTER YOUTH AND ADOPTEES

I'm often asked how I can be so strong after living through such a complicated adoption story and after dealing with such a deep depression while unwrapping my adoption trauma. The answer is that I had to prioritize my mental health. Now, although it sounds pretty simple, the process isn't quite so clean cut.

For the past ten years, I have been in and out of therapy and on and off medications. I've had great therapists and questionable ones. I've even had psychiatrists who threw cocktails of drugs at me when I was at my lowest and didn't care if these made me a shell of a person. It took a long time for me to find a doctor who actually listened and prioritized my health.

Therapy may not be a cure-all, but it can be a great tool for adoptees and adoptive parents who need to process trauma and other problems. Adoptive parents especially need to consider therapy so that they don't bring infertility grief, intergenerational trauma, or other problems into their parenting. Even if you think you have managed to deal appropriately up until now, you may be surprised at how helpful therapy can be for the whole family. And even if you think your adopted child is well adjusted, it can still be a good step in preventative action to make sure they have healthy tools and skills they can use to cope if they need them in the future (i.e., when they come out of the fog).

In this chapter, we will discuss the importance of mental health in adoptive families, and we will cover some tips to improve our mental health, some red flags to watch out for, the types of therapy, as well as input from a licensed, trauma-informed therapist. But before we begin, please answer the following two questions:

What are some ways you prioritize your mental health right now?

What are some barriers to you prioritizing your mental health?

MEET THE EXPERT: MARCELLA MOSLOW

Marcella Moslow is a licensed clinical social worker (LCSW) in the state of New York, a Registered Play Therapist (RPT), and has trained in the attachment-focused modality of Theraplay. Additionally, she is trained and is certified in Eye Movement Desensitization and Reprocessing (EMDR). Marcella is also trained in other trauma reprocessing modalities including Progressive Counting and Brainspotting. Further, she is certified in the Safe and Sound Protocol (SSP). She is also an adoptee.

Back in 2015 Marcella started working in this field by providing education and support to adoptive families and adoptees in various capacities. She has worked at a clinical level with adoptees and individuals in foster care as well as with their adoptive/foster/biological families in settings including outpatient mental health clinics, schools, and now in her own private practice. She is a trainer and educator for adoptive families and professionals working with adoptees and their families and provides parent consultations.

When I asked her what the biggest misconceptions are that she hears about adoption, Marcella said: 1) There is no trauma in adoption, 2) Adoption is giving a child a better life, and 3) Adoption is adoptee centered and focuses primarily on what is in the best interests of the child.

As an adoptee, I have firsthand experience with many misconceptions, and on my mental health journey, they have definitely affected my treatment by doctors who were not experts. Over the span of ten years, I've tried an array of therapies, and it took a long time to find a therapist who was right for me. I firmly believe that this was because many of the therapists I saw weren't adoption competent, which is why it is so essential to have experts like Marcella.

WHAT IS AN ADOPTION-COMPETENT THERAPIST?

According to Marcella, the term *adoption-competent therapist* is used by adoption agencies/organizations affiliated with adoption that have created certification programs for professionals that "certify" them as adoption competent after they have completed a certain amount of coursework. Although the adoption competency programs typically cover a variety of topics that do pertain to adoption and do provide some foundational information, they are by no means exhaustive. According to Marcella, topics vary based on the program; they do not delve into or require extensive knowledge on areas such as trauma, attachment, or neurobiology; and they are often taught by individuals without lived experience.

Finding the right therapist is very much like speed dating. You try to find out as much information as possible, set up an initial meeting, and then you either click or you struggle through sessions until you call it quits. Just like the dating process, it can take a bit of time and effort to find a therapist who is right for you or your child.

In a 2015 study by the American Psychological Association, 5.3 percent of psychologists are Black, 5 percent are Hispanic/Latinx, 4.3 percent are Asian, 1.7 percent classified themselves as "other," and an astounding 83.6 percent are white.[4] What does this mean for you? Well, for the average adoptive parent (who are majority white), it means they are more likely to find a therapist who can relate more easily to the struggles that they (the parents) go through. But for a BIPOC child, this can make finding a fit with a therapist even more difficult because of certain identity struggles, racism, and even economic differences that they experience that a white therapist can never fully understand.

Over the years I have found that many clinicians or professionals in the field use "adoption-competent" inappropriately and even utilize it or state that they "specialize" in adoption without adequate qualifications. What many do not know is that the nuances and intricacies of adoption are barely touched upon in most master's programs; many consider researching the subject as being enough to consider themselves competent. Some professionals get into the field who do not have backgrounds in helping support individuals and families with complex trauma. Additionally, some professionals bring their own biases or narratives about adoption to the table, which can harm the therapeutic process. These are not ethical practices and can lead to added trauma for the individual. Just remember that all types of therapy and all therapists are not equal.

FINDING AN EXPERIENCED ADOPTION THERAPIST FOR BIPOC

When seeking services, Marcella recommends that adoptees and their families seek out a trauma therapist who also has either lived experience or who has had extensive experience working with this population, rather than seeking out someone with only the title "adoption-competent therapist." A certified trauma therapist will have extensive training and understanding of developmental and attachment trauma, the neurobiological and somatic impacts of early trauma, and methods for helping clients to reprocess traumatic content. If an individual or family can also find a trauma therapist with lived experience and one who shares the same race as the adoptee, this is extremely beneficial, says Marcella.

Here are three tips that can make this process a little easier.

Search Directories of BIPOC and Adoption-Competent Mental Health Professionals

Whereas it can be difficult to find BIPOC or trauma-informed therapists, many different websites and resources can make the process a little easier. Check out these choices and start making a list of therapists in your area.

BIPOC THERAPIST

- Inclusive Therapists: A Safer, Simpler Way to Find Care, www .inclusivetherapists.com

- Latinx Therapists and Speakers, https://latinxtherapy.com

- Therapy for Black Girls, https://providers.therapyforblackgirls.com

- Melanin and Mental Health, www.melaninandmentalhealth.com

- Therapy for Black Men, https://therapyforblackmen.org

ADOPTION-COMPETENT THERAPIST

- Center for Adoption Support and Education (C.A.S.E.), Directory of TAC Trained Mental Health Professionals, https://tinyurl.com/t6vu88fv

- Adoptive and Foster Family Coalition, "Finding and Working with Adoption-Competent Therapists," by Claudia Corrigan D'Arcy, https://tinyurl.com/48vh5jc4

- Find an Adoption Therapist, www.psychologytoday.com/us/therapists/adoption

Prepare to Interview

Although many therapists look good on paper, it can be hard to tell which is a good fit just from the description on a website. To help increase the odds of a good match, you can ask some of the following questions.

- Are you licensed? What are your specialties?

- What insurance plans do you take, or do you offer sliding scale payments?

- What is your connection to adoption?

- Do you work with a diverse population or BIPOC children?

- Do your religious views affect your approach?

- How do you determine counseling goals?

- Is therapy in person, and are online sessions available?

- How many years of experience do you have working with adopted children?

- Are you qualified to prescribe medication? If not, do you work closely with psychiatrists when creating a treatment plan?

Be Open to Failure

When you're thinking about starting therapy for the first time it can be very easy to get overwhelmed; sometimes you may even worry that you're wasting your time or maybe even the therapist's. But it is important to know that failure can sometimes be a good thing. People can go into this journey thinking that they really would like one type of therapist or therapeutic approach and learn that it's just not right for them—and that's okay! Failure in this way can help you and your therapist learn what is right for you or help you know what qualities in a therapist help you the most.

If you are an adoptive parent helping your child find the right therapist, remember that failure is okay and encourage your child/teen to think of failure in this way as being a natural part of the process. Try asking the following questions to help with the process.

THERAPY FOLLOW-UP QUESTIONS:

- What did you like about this therapist?

- What did you think you'd like but didn't?

- What piqued your interest about a certain therapeutic approach?

- Did therapy help in any way?

- What did you learn from this experience that can help you moving forward?

RED FLAGS TO LOOK OUT FOR

Marcella encourages families to do their research and to ask lots of questions of potential therapists to ensure the therapist has the necessary qualifications and experience and is an appropriate fit. She advises families to be wary of therapists/providers who

- Disregard the fact that a child is adopted or do not acknowledge trauma

- Do not ask parents about a full medical history

- Say they don't work with a significant number of adoptees

- Do not have experience working with clients of a different race

- Have a one-sided view of adoption

- Emphasize diagnosing or pathologizing

- Immediately recommend medication

- Are affiliated with an adoption agency

- Place the adoptee in the position of having to provide education on adoption to the therapist

WHEN TO SEEK HELP

I recommend that all adoptive parents and adoptees establish a relationship with a therapist to have a baseline. From my experience, it is typically better to consult with a professional who can fill your toolbox with healthy coping mechanisms that you can rely on if you need to later on, rather than waiting for a serious problem to surface and doing damage control all at once.

When I asked Marcella about when adoptive parents should look for help, she recommended that they seek services for their child as soon as possible. She emphasized that processing traumatic content early can greatly reduce the lasting impacts of trauma on the brain and body. Adoptees are on a lifelong journey and will require different levels of support at each developmental stage they go through (for example, for many teens in treatment, there is a heavy focus on identify formation, for younger children the focus is more on building healthy attachments and helping regulate the nervous system, and for adults the focus is on how being adopted impacts their significant relationships). Based on where a client is developmentally, the approach to treatment and the modalities used may change, but trauma therapy can be administered at any age. Therapy also does not have to be constant; clients may work through a particular area and then need to reengage later because traumatic experiences manifest differently at individual ages. It is never too late to seek out services. That said, adoptive parents should be proactive and avoid waiting for "something bad" to happen as a reason to engage in therapy, Marcella added.

But what if a child seems "fine"? I hear this question from adoptive parents often. I'd like to remind every parent of their childhood and teen years and have them consider how open they were with their parents. Marcella adds that there is a common misconception that children who have experienced trauma are fine. This wording is typically used to describe children who do not outwardly display symptoms like aggression, self-harm, defiance, or other intense behaviors. The impacts of childhood trauma can be lifelong and manifest differently for each person. Those who are perceived as fine have developed a complex system of protective strategies/trauma responses/coping skills that fall into the area of what is considered socially acceptable. These are often the children who slip through the cracks and do not get the help they need, Marcella shares.

But how can you encourage children to see a therapist if they do not want to? When I asked Marcella this, she said that in her experience, if a child is resistant to therapy, it has to do with two factors.

1. The family lacks openness.

2. The child feels in need of protection.

When a family isn't openly discussing adoption and the child has not been a part of the conversation about therapy, it can feel as if they are being sent to the therapist to be "fixed." Families need to have open conversations about therapy and what it is for, and if age-appropriate, allow the child to be a part of the therapist finding process. Families also need to be able to have conversations about difficult topics without shaming, belittling, or becoming confrontational. The child's need for protection may present with the child appearing resistant, withdrawn, or opposed to services. If this occurs, the therapist may need to slow down and allot plenty of time to ensure that the child feels safe and secure in the therapeutic relationship; that way they can align with the client's protective system instead of fighting against it or trying to change it. For children, it is also important to find a therapist who has experience with play therapy since this is the way young children process and learn.

Marcella also adds that with trauma-informed/trauma therapy in particular, it is important to point out that yes, coping skills are important, but often they are not enough, and sometimes such mechanisms aren't reliable for individuals with complex trauma histories because coping skills require a lot of executive functioning skills that trauma can inhibit. This is why it is good for families to understand the impacts of trauma and how the trauma affects them currently, in addition to understanding the stabilizing symptoms that manifest and reduce the overall impacts of traumatic experience.

Warning Signs

While considering care, make sure you keep an eye out for some of the following red flags that show the need for more immediate care.[5]

Regressions

For younger children, regressions can be a cause for concern. Children can start bed-wetting after being fully potty trained, exhibit excessive anxiety, or even revert to baby talk when they are an older child.

Behavior Changes

Watch out for the following:

- Self-harm, skin-picking, or hair-pulling

- Comments like "Nobody would care if I weren't here."

- Significant changes in appetite or sleep

- Interest in or use of drugs/alcohol

- Risky sexual behavior

Isolation and Withdrawal

Pay attention when

- Younger children avoid playdates or activities in which other children are present and present a desire to stay home constantly.

- Older children push parents/peers away and or have more defiant behavior.

Talks about Suicide

The following signs should concern you:

- Starts giving away possessions

- Talks about a plan

If this happens, *seek immediate help from a professional and call one of these numbers*:

- 988 Suicide and Crisis line

- Text the Crisis Text Line (**text HOME to 741741**)

TYPES OF THERAPY

When you are thinking about starting therapy as an adoptive parent or you are choosing a therapist for a child or teen, it is important to have a general understanding of the types of therapy that are out there. Here are some of the approaches that Marcella recommends for developmental trauma:

BRAINSPOTTING This is an alternative therapy that uses visual spots to help a person process trauma and reset the body and brain. It was created by David Grand as an advancement to his work in EMDR therapy.[6] For more information on brainspotting or to find a certified clinician near you, go to https://brainspotting.com/.

THERAPLAY Theraplay is a type of dyadic child and family therapy that has been practiced around the world for over fifty years. Its goal is to help support a healthy child/caregiver attachment through play that is guided by a therapist.[7] For more information or to find a Theraplay provider near you, check out https://theraplay.org/.

INTERNAL FAMILY SYSTEMS (IFS) This is an approach to therapy that focuses on subpersonalities that a person has. Each subpersonality has different wounded parts that are dealing with painful emotions, and the goal is to heal each part and find balance.[8] For more information or to find an IFS provider near you, visit https://ifs-institute.com/.

SOMATIC EXPERIENCES This is another alternative therapy that focuses on healing or releasing trauma that is trapped in the body.[9]

EYE MOVEMENT DESENSITIZATION AND REPROCESSING THERAPY (EMDR) EMDR uses rhythmic left-right stimulation to help relieve emotions blocked by trauma.[10] For more information or to find a certified EMDR provider near you, visit https://www.emdria.org/.

Some other therapies that are commonly used are

COGNITIVE-BEHAVIORAL THERAPY (CBT) CBT addresses unhelpful thought problems or negative cognitions by identifying patterns with the help of your therapist.[11]

DIALECTICAL BEHAVIORAL THERAPY (DBT) DBT focuses on skills used in CBT but prioritizes emotional regulation and acceptance as well as practicing certain skills to use in difficult situations.[12]

DEVELOPMENTAL PSYCHOTHERAPY (DDP) Developed by Dan Hughes, DDP is based on the theoretical understanding of attachment in relationships and the impact of trauma. In this type of therapy, a therapist works on helping improve the child's relationship with their parents in a collaborative approach, first by working with the parents and actively preparing them. Parents will learn their role and how to explore the impact parenting has had on them and their attachment histories.

By addressing this, the therapist can help parents better understand their emotions and how to remain empathetic to their child during challenges. Once the therapist considers the parents ready, the child will then join the sessions and the group will openly discuss past and current trauma and help the child achieve safety within their family.[13]

PLAY THERAPY Play therapy is typically used when a trained therapist uses their skills to provide materials and facilitate a safe relationship with the child so they can share feelings, experiences, and behaviors. Since play is a typical part of most children's day-to-day life, it can be easier for some children to connect with a therapist this way versus verbalizing their emotions and reactions.[14] For more information or to find a play therapist near you, visit https://www.a4pt.org/.

TYPES OF SOCIAL SUPPORT

When I asked Marcella what types of social support she'd recommend, she replied by saying that she highly recommends that both adoptees and adoptive parents seek their own therapy, their own support groups, and that they look into training/education opportunities. She suggests that caregivers should seek therapy services for themselves at all stages of the adoption process (before, during, and after) and encourage adoptees and adoptive parents to look into adoptee-centered social media pages, podcasts, and literature.

Here are her recommendations:

- Ask Adoption, "Connect-Discover-Heal" (AskAdoption.com)

- Beyond Words Psychological Services (growbeyondwords.com)

- Intercountry Adoptee Voices (ICAV), "Embrace the Lifelong Path" (https://intercountryadopteevoices.com/)

- Adoptees Connect, Where Adoptee Voices Meet—An Adoptee Centric Connect Group (adopteesconnect.com)

The following are some other non-adoptee resources she recommends:

- *Brain-Body Parenting: How to Stop Managing Behavior and Start Raising Joyful, Resilient Kids*, by Mona Delahooke

- *Parenting from the Inside Out: How a Deeper Self-Understanding Can Help You Raise Children Who Thrive*, by Daniel Siegel and Mary Hartzell

- *The Whole-Brain Child: 12 Revolutionary Strategies to Nurture Your Child's Developing Mind*, by Daniel J. Siegel and Tine Payne Bryson

- *The Body Keeps the Score: Brain, Mind and Body in the Healing of Trauma,* by Bessel van der Kolk

- *So You Want to Talk About Race,* by Ijeoma Oluo

- *White Fragility: Why It's So Hard for White People to Talk about Racism,* by Robin DiAngelo

- Any books/articles written by adoptees

- *Adoptees On* podcast

- Robyn Gobbel (https://robyngobbel.com/)

MARCELLA MOSLOW'S TOP FIVE TIPS FOR PARENTS

Marcella's many years of lived experience and work as a therapist have given her significant insight; she has a few great tips for parents that she loves to share.

1. Do your own work as an adoptive caregiver before, during, and after the adoption process is completed. It will not make things perfect or even easy, but it will make things easier. It's not up to your child to fix things on their own.

   Here are some actions you can take to improve/maintain your mental health:[15]

   ▸ Maintain a consistent sleep schedule.

   ▸ Exercise regularly.

   ▸ Drink and eat a balanced diet.

   ▸ Connect with your friends and family.

   ▸ Keep track of things that you are grateful for.

   ▸ Incorporate daily meditation or mindfulness.

2. Remember that your child's behavior is often the only way they can communicate what they need. Learn your child's cues and needs so that you can be a safe base for them.

3. Seek out individuals with lived experience and be willing and open to listening and learning from them. They can shed so much light on what your child may be experiencing and what's to come.

4. If you are a transracial family, seek out racial/cultural mirrors for your child.

5. Do your due diligence when finding providers for your child and family to make sure they have experience and expertise and are a good fit for your family. Don't settle; you risk the work being less effective.

MENTAL HEALTH TOOLS AND ACTIVITIES

When thinking about how to take care of your mental health, it is helpful to have several different tools and activities that you can rely on. Here are a few to consider using.

SCRAMBLE YOUR SENSES

One of my favorite grounding exercises that you may have heard of is the perfect tool for people of any age. Think about or write down. . .

- Five things you can **see**

- Four things you can **touch**

- Three things you can **feel**

- Two things you can **smell**

- One thing you can **taste**

REST AND REGULATION SPACE

Whether you are a child, teen, or adult, it is important to have a comfortable and safe place where you can go to be alone with your thoughts or to be with others depending on your preference. Whether a person is overwhelmed or simply wants to be alone, having a specific place with tools available can encourage them to coregulate.

Here are some great additions that you can purchase online:

- Sensory swing

- Bean bag chair

- Harkla Hug

- Weighted blanket or pad

- Sensory body sock or cocoon

- Pillows

- Punching bag

- Small trampoline

> NOTE Another easy way to bring yourself into the moment either on your own or with a child/teen is to play Categories. Choose a category (types of animals, colors, kinds of candy) and in your mind or out loud list as many as you can. No repeats or you have to start over.

> NOTE Body scans are another really useful way to increase our brain-body connection or get our brain and body to communicate to get what we need (this is something that those with early trauma struggle with). Either on your own or alongside your child, take a couple moments and scan your body from head to toe; simply notice and verbalize a sensation/emotion/thought that comes up.

CHAPTER 5 REFLECTION QUESTIONS

- How do you feel about therapy?

- How long are you willing to go to therapy for yourself?

- Have you been to therapy before?

- Do you have experience with children with trauma or mental illness?

- What type of therapy does your insurance cover? Can you afford out-of-network services if you need them?

- How do you feel about children receiving psychiatric medication?

- Are you prepared to take time off work to take your child back and forth to appointments if you need to?

- Do you have a support network?

6

ADDITIONAL RESOURCES AND MORE

If you are a prospective adoptive or foster parent or a current foster/adoptive parent, I would like to take the time to thank you for *doing the work*.

Ten years ago, if you had told me that educating adoptive parents would be such a huge part of my day-to-day work, I wouldn't have believed you. Speaking about adoption was a huge taboo subject in my family, and for years, I didn't have a community to support me. It wasn't until I started engaging more online with adoptees that I truly learned the power of sharing our stories and the nuances of adoption.

And in that beauty, I also found strength and healing in helping adoptive parents prepare for and support their children. If you are a parent who is willing to make mistakes, get uncomfortable, and try again, know that you are making a difference in a child's life.

The reason my mom and I have such a great relationship now is because she did the work. We both did. I was vulnerable, she was too, and we listened to each other, truly listened to one another, and that inspired her to learn more about adoption. She read my work, my book, and took the initiative to ask questions when she wasn't sure.

Adoptive parents don't have to be perfect. That's not what I or many adoptees are asking for. But just like parents expect children to own up to mistakes and do better, most of us expect the same of our adoptive parents.

Let's not pretend adoptive parents and the adoption industry are infallible.

Let's acknowledge the *real* history; let's acknowledge the pain and trauma that have been perpetuated by adoptive parents ignoring the issues and dumping more money into the industry instead of using their privilege and the powerful system to work with adoptees, birth parents, and former foster youth to make things better.

It's way past time for change.

Adoptees deserve love, a safe home, family, and community, and together we can work to make our families and communities that healthy space.

I would like to end this workbook with one last bit of support by sharing a piece of my mom's story and those of two other adoptive parents who have and continue to step up.

So, let's get to it.

ADOPTIVE PARENT STORIES

PAIGE KNIPFER, ADOPTIVE MOTHER

Hello. I'm an adoptive parent seven years in.

First, I'll start off by saying I'm always learning, and anyone involved needs to keep that mentality. We are ever evolving, learning, and, hopefully, growing generationally in adoption.

In the beginning stages of adoption, I admit I had many misconceptions. First and foremost, I had traveled internationally and visited orphanages. I had preconceived ideas about adoption in the United States and wrong ideas that I blame on movies and television. I thought adoptive parents were needed and didn't fully understand the trauma for the adoptee and the complexities of a person in crisis making an adoption plan. I didn't understand the adoption process, the state law differences, and being completely honest, the somewhat nonsensical/backward steps to adopt.

I wish I would have understood that the "check boxes" allow a social worker to discuss those items with you. It does not mean you have any control over anything. Prospective families should understand that you are essentially being trained to help walk your future child through all that comes up (medical, family history, connection to biology, trauma, etc.). Biology or not, your goal is to help this person become who they were meant to be and the best version of themselves. You are not to mold this child into who you want them to be, and that goes for sexual orientation, gender identity, career, interests, and so on.

We wanted to adopt because I couldn't have biological children. We wanted to be parents. I will say one thing I did well is properly grieve my infertility. Our relationship/marriage only grew as we had deeper conversations on whether biology was important, and we focused on our desire to be parents. I now work with prospective adoptive parents, and I often see parents who have not properly processed their prior journey before they begin the adoption journey. Adoption does not fill that void; it only magnifies cracks in yourself and your relationship/marriage. Work on your own traumas, grief, and marital issues before pursuing adoption.

I admit open adoption scared me. I envisioned the expecting mom changing her mind but being unable to do so. I envisioned her wanting to co-parent or make parenting decisions with us. In reality, it is nothing like either of those two things. I also didn't think about the complexities of including extended family members, the role addiction or poverty may play into navigating an open adoption, the feelings of the adoptee, of the birth family, and the seasons of life we all go through to make relationships work. It takes time, energy, and effort, but I now fully understand its importance. I try as much as I can to put myself in other shoes, and although I'll never be a birth parent or an adoptee, I try to think from those perspectives. I try to listen to so many different perspectives because every person is different and has a valued experience.

I also don't think I was ever properly prepared for adoption. We received no transracial adoption or exposure/long-term education. I wish I listened more to adoptees and birth parents' perspectives in the beginning. I wish I questioned the "professionals" more. I blindly trusted they had the best intentions and didn't fully see the corruption that can exist. I wish I pushed for birth father identification, to verify counseling and attorney representation for the expecting parent, to know how payment was taking place, and so on. I didn't even think to ask about so many things in the process. I wish an open adoption agreement was discussed and that it included social media, expectations, and a base for our relationship. I think an agreement would have only helped the beginning of our relationship. As a prospective adoptive parent, you think you have time for education or that certain education won't apply to you, but it might, so you should take in as much as you can. "The wait" seems to be the most difficult, but this is the time when you should consume and prepare as much as you can. This means thinking about how you will weave in your child's culture, what recipes/traditions you might incorporate, how you will navigate an open adoption, how you will approach questions from strangers, and how you will deal with medical or health unknowns.

I went from being completely oblivious to my role in adoption, to being guilt-ridden and feeling isolated, to, now, sitting in, understanding, always learning, and advocacy. I now recognize I'm a part of the trauma of adoption. I'm the one out of this who gains, unlike the adoptee and birth family. I feel like my relationship with my children has grown with my own growth as a person, parent, and in my adoption role. Our relationship with the birth family has evolved, and I have better compassion as well.

BETH CHRISTENSEN, ADOPTIVE MOTHER

My husband and I are the parents of two daughters from Asia: one born in China in 1995, and the other born in Vietnam in 1996. We adopted both as infants, and they are closely connected as sisters in our adoptive family.

As parents in general, we could have done a better job every day in countless ways. What parent doesn't feel this way?

As adoptive parents, a few regrets resonate strongly because of our status as an interracial family comprised of white parents with Asian daughters in a small Midwestern town.

Quite simply, we didn't talk about race enough.

Despite consistently celebrating our daughters' Asian traditions and holidays, we failed to incorporate discussions of racial inequity into our dinner table conversations. Our daily "check-in" discussions about each of our highs and lows of the day did not specifically focus on the difficult, often uncomfortable, topic of race often enough, and we regret this lapse.

But there are also things I believe we did well as a family. Foremost was to establish a network of other adoptive families. We developed a moderately large group of adoptive family friends—families that looked like us, with Asian children and white parents. It modeled and normalized our demographic. In addition to annual culture camps and other organized get-togethers, we fostered close informal friendships with those remarkable families. This was our place of belonging. We understood one another.

We traveled together for homeland tours when each of our daughters turned ten; and we gratefully continue to enjoy enduring relationships as both parents and adoptees with these families.

I realize that our journey is not simple. It is collective. Following the recent spate of anti-Asian hate crimes, I confessed to our oldest daughter that I felt guilty about putting her in the situation of being an Asian in the United States. She quickly reminded me that, "I guess the other option would have been growing up in a country with a political dictatorship: and how do you think that would have gone?" Bingo. Our independently minded political science major nailed the complexity of it all in that one question.

My husband and I have shared the bounty of our love and culture with two amazing human beings who bring determination and definition to our lives and, ultimately, to our country and democracy. As I consider the many imperfect ways in which our human lives intersect, I am proud to have been a part of this journey of grief, anger, strength, identity, and—ultimately—hope.

ADDITIONAL RESOURCES

NOTE I recommend watching/reading these with your child. It is a great way to model that these topics are safe to talk about, and it naturally opens up the opportunity for dialogue.

DIVERSE MOVIES AND TV SHOWS FOR YOUNGER CHILDREN

- *Encanto*
- *Dora the Explorer*
- *Go, Diego, Go*
- *Doc McStuffins*
- *Coco*
- *Moana*
- *BookMarks: Celebrating Black Voices*
- *Akeela and the Bee*
- *Spelling the Dream*
- *Raya and the Last Dragon*
- *Mira, Royal Detective*
- *Sophia the First*
- *Nella the Princess Knight*
- *Motown Magic*
- *Handy Manny*

DIVERSE MOVIES AND TV SHOWS FOR OLDER CHILDREN

- *One Day at a Time*
- *Gentefied*
- *Black Panther*
- *Jane the Virgin*
- *To All the Boys I Loved Before*
- *All Together Now*
- *Hidden Figures*
- *The Hate U Give*
- *Black-ish*

- *Fresh Off the Boat*
- *Spider-Man: Into the Spider-Verse*
- *A Ballerina's Tale*

NOTE *Books that are starred are written by adoptees or former foster youth.

ADOPTION BOOKS FOR KIDS

- *All Kinds of Families*, by Suzanne Lang
- *And Tango Makes Three*, by Justin Richardson and Peter Parnell
- *And That's Why She's My Mama*, by Tiarra Nazario
- *Coco & Olive: The Color of Love*, by Michelle Madrid-Branch*
- *The Family Book*, by Todd Parr
- *A Mother for Choco*, by Keiko Kasza
- *Stellaluna*, by Janell Cannon
- *Being Adopted*, by Amy Wilkerson*
- *You Weren't with Me*, by Chandra Ghosh Ippen
- *Forever Fingerprints*, by Sherrie Eldridge*
- *A Kids Book about Adoption*, by Leul Gurske and Nabil Zerizef*
- *Adoption Is a Lifelong Journey*, by Kelly DiBenedetto, Katie Gorczyca, and Jennifer Eckert
- *What Is Adoption?* by Jeanette Yoffe*
- *Let's Talk about It: Adoption*, by Fred Rogers
- *Adoption Is Both*, by Elena S. Hall*

ADOPTION BOOKS FOR ADULTS

- *All You Can Ever Know: A Memoir*, by Nicole Chung*
- *American Baby: A Mother, a Child, and the Shadow History of Adoption*, by Gabrielle Glaser

- *The Baby Scoop Era: Unwed Mothers, Infant Adoption, and Forced Surrender*, by Karen Wilson-Buterbaugh*

- *Bitterroot: A Salish Memoir of Transracial Adoption*, by Susan Devan Harness*

- *For Black Girls Like Me*, by Mariama J. Lockington*

- *The Girls Who Went Away: The Hidden History of Women Who Surrendered Children for Adoption in the Decades Before Roe v. Wade*, by Ann Fessler*

- *Growing Up Black in White*, by Kevin D. Hofmann*

- *Inconvenient Daughter*, by Lauren J. Sharkey*

- *In Their Voices: Black Americans on Transracial Adoption*, by Rhonda M. Roorda*

- *The Lived Experiences of Colombian Adoptees*, edited by Abby Forero-Hilty*

- *A Long Way Home: A Memoir*, by Saroo Brierley*

- *Lucky Girl*, by Mei-Ling Hopgood*

- *Motherhood So White: A Memoir of Race, Gender, and Parenting in America*, by Nefertiti Austin

- *Not My White Savior: A Memoir in Poems*, by Julayane Lee*

- *Older Sister. Not Necessarily Related. A Memoir*, by Jenny Heijun Wills*

- *Palimpsest: Documents from a Korean Adoption*, by Lisa Wool-Rim Sjöblom*

- *The Primal Wound*, by Nancy Newton Verrier

- *A Princess Found: An American Family, an African Chiefdom, and the Daughter Who Connected Them All*, by Sarah Culberson* and Tracy Trivas

- *Searching for Mom: A Memoir*, by Sara Easterly*

- *See No Color*, by Shannon Gibney*

- *Selling Transracial Adoption: Families, Markets, and the Color Line*, by Elizabeth Raleigh*

- *Set Free: A Childhood Memoir*, by Destini McAlister*

- *Surviving the White Gaze: A Memoir*, by Rebecca Carroll*

- *Through Adopted Eyes: A Collection of Memoirs from Adoptees*, by Elena S. Hall*

- *Welcome Home: An Anthology on Love and Adoption*, by Eric Smith*

- *Ward of the State*, by Karlos Dillard*

- *The Son with Two Moms*, by Anthony Hynes*

- *Three Little Words: A Memoir,* by Ashley Rhodes-Courter*

- *The Child Catchers: Rescue, Trafficking, and the New Gospel of Adoption*, by Kathryn Joyce

- *Confessions of a Lost Mother*, by Elisa M. Barton

- *Birth Fathers and Their Adoption Experiences*, by Gary Clapton

- *Surrender: A Memoir of Nature, Nurture, and Love*, by Marylee MacDonald

- *Prison Baby: A Memoir*, by Deborah Jiang Stein

- *Heart and Seoul*, by Jen Frederick

- *Jagged Little Pill: The Novel*, by Eric Smith, Alanis Morissette, Diablo Cody, and Glen Ballard

- *Everyone Was Falling*, by JS Lee

DIVERSE BOOKS FOR KIDS

- *Alma and How She Got Her Name*, by Juana Martinez-Neal

- *Bad Hair Does Not Exist! Pelo Malo No Existe!*, by Sulma Arzu-Brown

- *The Colors of Us*, by Karen Katz

- *Dreamers*, by Yuyi Morales

- *From North to South/Del Norte al Sur*, by René Colato Laínez

- *Happy in Our Skin*, by Fran Manushkin

- *I Am Enough*, by Grace Byers

- *Islandborn*, by Junot Díaz

- *Little Legends: Bold Women in Black History*, by Vashti Harrison

- *Love Makes a Family*, by Sophie Beer

- *Sulwe*, by Lupita Nyong'o

- *Think Big, Little One*, by Vashti Harrison

BOOKS ON ANTI-RACISM

- *Between the World and Me*, by Ta-Nehisi Coates

- *The Color of Law: A Forgotten History of How Our Government Segregated America*, by Richard Rothstein

- *How to Be an Antiracist*, by Ibram X. Kendi

- *Inventing Latinos: A New Story of American Racism*, by Laura E. Gómez

- *Just Mercy: A Story of Justice and Redemption*, by Bryan Stevenson

- *Me and White Supremacy*, by Layla F. Saad

- *The New Jim Crow: Mass Incarceration in the Age of Colorblindness*, by Michelle Alexander

- *Racism without Racists: Color-Blind Racism and the Persistence of Racial Inequality*, by Eduardo Bonilla-Silva

- *Raising White Kids: Bringing Up Children in a Racially Unjust America*, by Jennifer Harvey

- *So You Want to Talk About Race*, by Ijeoma Oluo

FINAL DISCUSSION QUESTIONS

What was your favorite section?

What did you find most challenging?

When you hear criticism about other adoptive parents from adoptees, how do you feel after working through this book?

LEVEL UP Where do you notice those emotions in your body? Recall other instances in your life where you have experienced those same emotions and body sensations, and reflect on what comes up.

Are you worried that criticisms about adoption reflect criticisms of your own parenting? Why or why not? Why do you think it's sometimes easier to defend other adoptive parents instead of validating the lived experiences of adoptees?

What are some ethical issues with the adoption industry?

In what ways does adoption function as an industry? What social and economic structures support it, and how can this knowledge inform positive change in the industry?

What is the transracial adoption paradox? How does it show up in your family? In society or the media?

What is toxic positivity?

How does toxic positivity apply to adoptive parents or the adoption industry? What impacts can it have on adoptees' experiences, happiness, and mental health?

What is colorism?

What does it mean to come "out of the fog"?

If you're an adoptive parent, how have you integrated nuance and complexity into your understanding of adoption? How can you support your child as they come "out of the fog"? How have your own thoughts about the picture-perfect adoption story shifted as you've read this book?

What stories do you usually see about adoption on your social media, in the news, or from folks in your community? Are they always positive?

If you only see/hear positive stories, what might those narratives be glossing over? Have you heard stories from adoptees that aren't so positive? What did they say, and how did you react? Why?

What is the savior mentality? What characteristics define a white savior?

Have you ever felt that you were called to "save" via adoption? How is this mentality harmful to adoptees?

What does the white savior mentality reflect about the adoption industry? What does it reflect about our culture at large?

What kinds of situations might cause a family to consider placing their child for adoption? What other ways can we support keeping families together?

Can you think of a time when something you said, did, or assumed revealed an unconscious bias? Did your child point it out to you, or did you realize it on your own? What did you do, and how can you do better next time?

What is a microaggression?

What is a microassault? What is a microinvalidation?

How can each show up in your family?

Have you ever said that you "don't see color"? Why or why not?

If you have, what signal did you intend to send? What implications could that have for kids of color living in a world that treats them differently because of their racial or ethnic identity? Why is it important to "see" race, and how might this help your child feel safe, seen, and validated?

Will you share your adoptive child's story in the future? If so, what attributes or experience do you focus on?

NOTES

1 Konstantin Lukin, "Toxic Positivity: Don't Always Look on the Bright Side," *The Man Cave* (blog), *Psychology Today*, August 1, 2019, www.psychologytoday.com/us/blog/the -man-cave/201908/toxic-positivity-dont-always-look-the-bright-side.

2 Marietta E. Spencer, "The Terminology of Adoption," *Child Welfare* 58, no. 7 (July–August 1979): 451–459.

3 Anonymous response by adoptive parent to survey conducted by the author, May 20, 2020.

4 Tami (@talck1966), "Adoptees: Which adoption term are you most triggered by and want to see it gone?" Twitter thread, June 23, 2020, https://twitter.com/talck1966/status /1275550673707253760.

5 Kathryn A Sweeney, "Race-Conscious Adoption Choices, Multiraciality, and Color-Blind Racial Ideology," *Family Relations: An Interdisciplinary Journal of Applied Family Studies* 62, no. 1 (February 2013): 42–57, https://doi.org/10.1111/j.1741-3729.2012.00757.x.

6 Michele Goodwin, "The Free-Market Approach to Adoption: The Value of a Baby," *Boston College Third World Law Journal* 26, no. 1 (2006), http://lawdigitalcommons.bc.edu/twlj /vol26/iss1/5.

7 Madeline Engel, Norma Phillips, and Frances Della Cava, "Inter-Country Adoption of Children Born in the United States," *Sociology between the Gaps: Forgotten and Neglected Topics* 1, no. 1 (March 2015), https://digitalcommons.providence.edu/cgi/viewcontent .cgi?article=1000&context=sbg.

8 *Merriam-Webster.com*, s. v. "colorism," accessed February 15, 2021, www.merriam-webster .com/dictionary/colorism.

9 Sweeney, "Race-Conscious Adoption Choices," 42–57.

10 Pamela Anne Quiroz, "Latino and Asian Infant Adoption: From Mongrels to 'Honorary White' or White?" *Journal of Latino-Latin American Studies (JOLLAS)* 2, no. 3 (2007): 46–58, https://doi.org/10.18085/llas.2.3.43qv4p04t4277136.

11 Quiroz, "Latino and Asian Infant Adoption," 46–58.

12 Nicholas Levy, Cindy Harmon-Jones, and Eddie Harmon-Jones, "Dissonance and Discomfort: Does a Simple Cognitive Inconsistency Evoke a Negative Affective State?" *Motivation Science* 4, no. 2 (2018): 95–108, https://doi.org/10.1037/mot0000079.

13 Susan Burke, Glen Schmidt, Shannon Wagner, Ross Hoffman, and Neil Hanlon, "Cognitive Dissonance in Social Work," *Journal of Public Child Welfare* 11, no. 3 (February 2017): 299–317, https://doi.org/10.1080/15548732.2016.1278068.

14 Engel, Phillips, and Della Cava, "Inter-Country Adoption of the United States."

15 @adoptee_thoughts, Twitter screenshot of @guidarichards, July 15, 2022, www.instagram .com/p/CgCRO2puxJb/?utm_source=ig_web_copy_link.

16 Department of Economic and Social Affairs, *Child Adoption: Trends and Policies* (New York: United Nations, 2009), 1–486, www.un.org/en/development/desa/population/publications /pdf/policy/child-adoption.pdf.

17 Patricia K Jennings, "The Trouble with the Multiethnic Placement Act: An Empirical Look at Transracial Adoption," *Sociological Perspectives* 49, no. 4 (December 2006): 559–81, https:// doi.org/10.1525/sop.2006.49.4.559.

18 Elizabeth Bartholet, "International Adoption, the Human Rights Position," *Global Policy* 1, no. 1 (January 2010): 91–100, https://doi.org/10.1111/j.1758-5899.2009.00001.x.

19 Department of Economic and Social Affairs, *Child Adoption*, 1–486.

20 Victor Groza and Kelley McCreery Bunkers, "The United States as a Sending Country for Intercountry Adoption: Birth Parents' Rights versus the 1993 Hague Convention on Inter-country Adoption," *Adoption Quarterly* 17, no. 1 (2014): 44–64, http://doi.org/10.1080 /10926755.2014.875089.

21 Joan Heifetz Hollinger, "Overview of the Multiethnic Placement Act (MEPA)," Ct.gov, 2006–2007, www.ct.gov/ccpa/lib/ccpa/MEPA_(Multi-Ethnic_Placement_Act).pdf.

22 Jennings, "Trouble with Multiethnic Placement Act," 559–81.

23 Mary Annette Pember, "Death by Civilization," *The Atlantic*, March 8, 2019, www .theatlantic.com/education/archive/2019/03/traumatic-legacy-indian-boarding-schools/584293/.

24 "Setting the Record Straight: The Indian Child Welfare Act Fact Sheet," National Indian Child Welfare Association, September 2015, www.nicwa.org/wp-content/uploads/2017/04 /Setting-the-Record-Straight-ICWA-Fact-Sheet.pdf.

25 Leah Litman and Matthew L.M. Fletcher, "The Necessity of the Indian Child Welfare Act," *The Atlantic*, January 22, 2020, www.theatlantic.com/ideas/archive/2020/01/fifth-circuit -icwa/605167/.

26 Nancy Marie Spears, "How an Ojibwe Grandmother's Adoption Fight in Minnesota Ended Up in the U.S. Supreme Court. *Sahan Journal*. October 20, 2022, https://sahanjournal.com/policing -justice/brackeen-v-haaland-native-adoption-us-supreme-court-minnesota-bradshaw-icwa/.

27 Travel.State.Gov, "Understanding the Hague Convention," US Department of State: Bureau of Consular Affairs, accessed February 16, 2021, https://travel.state.gov/content/travel/en /Intercountry-Adoption/Adoption-Process/understanding-the-hague-convention.html.

28 Sweeney, "Race-Conscious Adoption Choices," 42–57.

29 Gina Miranda Samuels, "'Being Raised by White People': Navigating Racial Difference among Adopted Multiracial Adults," *Journal of Marriage and Family* 71, no.1 (January 27, 2009): 80–94, https://doi.org/10.1111/j.1741-3737.2008.00581.x.

30 Samuels, "Being Raised by White People," 80–94.

31 Allon Kalisher, Jennah Gosciak, and Jill Spielfogel, "The Multiethnic Placement Act 25 Years Later: Trends in Adoption and Transracial Adoption," Office of the Assistant Secretary for Planning and Evaluation, US Department of Health and Human Services, December 2020, https://aspe.hhs.gov/sites/default/files/private/pdf/264526/MEPA-Data-report.pdf.

32 NPR Staff, "Six Words: 'Black Babies Cost Less to Adopt," National Public Radio: Morning Edition, June 27, 2013, www.npr.org/2013/06/27/195967886/six-words-black-babies-cost -less-to-adopt.

33 Sophie Brown, "Overseas Adoptions Rise—For Black American Children," *CNN*, September 17, 2013, www.cnn.com/2013/09/16/world/international-adoption-us-children-adopted -abroad/.

34 Brown, "Overseas Adoptions Rise."

35 Don Lash, "Race and Class in the US Foster Care System," *International Socialist Review* 91, (Winter 2013–14), https://isreview.org/issue/91/race-and-class-us-foster-care-system.

36 Joshua B. Padilla, Jose H. Vargas, and H. Lyssette Chavez, "Influence of Age on Transracial Foster Adoptions and Its Relation to Ethnic Identity Development," *Adoption Quarterly* 13, no. 1 (2010): 50–73, https://doi.org/10.1080/10926751003662598.

37 Padilla, Vargas, and Chavez, "Influence of Age on Transracial Foster Adoptions," 50–73.

38 Padilla, Vargas, and Chavez, "Influence of Age on Transracial Foster Adoptions," 50–73.

39 Susan Chibnall, "Children of Color in the Child Welfare System: Perspectives from the Child Welfare Community," Howard University School of Social Work, December 2003, www .childwelfare.gov/pubpdfs/children.pdf.

40 Malika Saar, Rebecca Epstein, Lindsay Rosenthal, and Yasmin Vafa, *The Sexual Abuse to Prison Pipeline: The Girls' Story*, Human Rights Project for Girls (Washington, DC: Center on Poverty and Equality/Georgetown Law, February 10, 2018), https://rights4girls.org /wp-content/uploads/2020/11/SexualAbusetoPrisonPipeline-Report.pdf.

Chapter 2

1 Elizabeth Raleigh, "Conclusion: The Consequences of Selling Transracial Adoption and the Implications for Adoptive Families," In *Selling Transracial Adoption: Families, Markets, and the Color Line* (Philadelphia: Temple University Press, 2018), 190–202, https://doi .org/10.2307/j.ctt21216x4.10.

2 Olusesan Ayodeji Makinde, "Infant Trafficking and Baby Factories: A New Tale of Child Abuse in Nigeria," *Child Abuse Review* 25, no. 6 (November/December 2016): 433–43, https://doi.org/10.1002/car.2420.

3 OHCHR, "Illegal Adoptions," United Nations Office of the High Commissioner Human Rights, accessed February 18, 2021, https://www.ohchr.org/EN/Issues/Children/Pages /Illegaladoptions.aspx.

4 Adoption Triad, "Unregulated Custody Transfer of Adopted Children," Administration for Children and Families, US Department of Health and Human Services, August 2019, www .childwelfare.gov/news-events/adoptiontriad/editions/aug2019/.

5 Melissa Guida-Richards, "I Was Adopted Outside of the US and Have Disabilities. I'm Tired of the Savior Narrative among White Adoptive Parents," *Insider*, June 3, 2020, https://www .insider.com/im-an-adoptee-im-tired-white-saviors-like-myka-stauffer-2020-6.

6 Child Welfare Information Gateway, "Adoption Disruption and Dissolution," Children's Bureau/ACYF *Numbers and Trends*, June 2012, www.childwelfare.gov/pubpdfs/ s_disrup.pdf.

7 Jenn Morson, "When Families Un-adopt a Child," *The Atlantic*, November 16, 2018, www .theatlantic.com/family/archive/2018/11/children-who-have-second-adoptions/575902/.

8 "Child Welfare Information Gateway, "Adoption Disruption and Dissolution."

9 Ann Fessler, *The Girls Who Went Away: The Hidden History of Women Who Surrendered Children for Adoption in the Decades before Roe v. Wade* (New York: Penguin Press, 2007).

10 Rachel Martin and NPR Staff, "Remembering the Doomed First Flight of Operation Baby-lift," *NPR*, April 26, 2015, www.npr.org/2015/04/26/402208267/remembering-the-doomed-first-flight-of-operation-babylift.

11 PBS, "Daughter from Danang: Operation Babylift (1975)," *PBS: American Experience*, accessed February 18, 2021, www.pbs.org/wgbh/americanexperience/features/daughter-operation-babylift-1975/.

12 PBS, "Daughter from Danang."

13 Makinde, "Infant Trafficking and Baby Factories," 433–43.

14 Lindsay Whitehurst, "Paul Petersen Pleads Guilty to Human Smuggling in Adoption Scheme," FOX 10 Phoenix, June 19, 2020, www.fox10phoenix.com/news/paul-petersen-pleads-guilty-to-human-smuggling-in-adoption-scheme.

15 Jessica Boehm and Robert Anglen, "'A Baby-Selling Enterprise': Former Arizona Elected Official Sentenced to 6-Plus Years in Adoption Scheme," *USA Today*, December 2, 2020, www.usatoday.com/story/news/nation/2020/12/01/paul-petersen-sentenced-6-plus-years-adoption-scheme/3786156001/.

16 Teo Armus and Maria Sacchetti, "The Parents of 545 Children Separated at the Border Still Haven't Been Found. The Pandemic Isn't Helping," *Washington Post*, October 22, 2020, www.washingtonpost.com/nation/2020/10/21/family-separation-parents-border-covid/.

17 Camilo Montoya-Galvez, "U.S. Shelters Received a Record 122,000 Unaccompanied Migrant Children in 2021," *CBS News*, December 23, 2021, www.cbsnews.com/news/immigration-122000-unaccompanied-migrant-children-us-shelters-2021/.

18 Armus and Sacchetti, "The Parents of 545 Children."

19 Associated Press, "Deported Parents May Lose Kids to Adoption, Investigation Finds," NBC-News.com, October 10, 2018, https://www.nbcnews.com/news/latino/deported-parents-may-lose-kids-adoption-investigation-finds-n918261.

20 The Associated Press, "Deported Parents May Lose Kids."

21 Dahlia Lithwick, "The Horrifying Implications of Alito's Most Alarming Footnote." *Slate*, May 10, 2022, https://slate.com/news-and-politics/2022/05/the-alarming-implications-of-alitos-domestic-supply-of-infants-footnote.html.

22 Sydney Trent, "Women Denied Abortion Rarely Choose Adoption. That's Unlikely to Change," *The Washington Post*, July 18, 2022, www.washingtonpost.com/dc-md-va/2022/07/18/adoption-abortion-roe-dobbs/.

Chapter 3

1   Kristen Pauker, Amanda Williams, and Jennifer Steele, "Children's Racial Categorization in Context," *Child Development Perspectives* 10, no. 1 (March 2016): 33–38, https://doi.org/10.1111/cdep.12155.

2   Helen A. Neville, Miguel E. Gallardo, and Derald Wing Sue, "Introduction: Has the United States Really Moved Beyond Race?" in *The Myth of Racial Color Blindness: Manifestations, Dynamics, and Impact* edited by H. A. Neville, M. E. Gallardo, and D. W. Sue (eds) (American Psychological Association, 2016), 3–21, https://doi.org/10.1037/14754-001.

3   Kevin L. Nadal, Katie E. Griffin, Yinglee Wong, Sahran Hamit, and Morgan Rasmus, "The Impact of Racial Microaggressions on Mental Health: Counseling Implications for Clients of

Color," *Journal of Counseling and Development* 92, no. 1 (January 2014): 57–66, https://doi
.org/10.1002/j.1556-6676.2014.00130.x.

4 Sumie Okazaki, "Impact of Racism on Ethnic Minority Mental Health," *Perspectives on Psychological Science* 4, no. 1 (January 2009): 103–07, www.jstor.org /stable/40212301.

5 Elena Rivera, "Lack of Therapists of Color Creates Barriers to Mental Health Access," WFAE
90.7: Charlotte's NPR News Source, July 24, 2019, www.wfae.org/local-news/2019-07-24
/lack-of-therapists-of-color-creates-barriers-to-mental-health-access.

6 Rivera, "Lack of Therapists of Color."

7 Rivera, "Lack of Therapists of Color."

8 CDC, "Working Together to Reduce Black Maternal Mortality," Centers for Disease Control
and Prevention, April 6, 2022), www.cdc.gov/healthequity/features/maternal-mortality/index
.html.

9 Salma Abdelnour Gilman, "Too Many Doctors Are Misdiagnosing Disease on Skin of Color,"
EverydayHealth.com, September 27, 2021, /www.everydayhealth.com/black-health
/too-many-doctors-are-misdiagnosing-disease-on-skin-of-color/.

10 Janice A. Sabin, "How We Fail Black Patients in Pain," AAMC, January 6, 2020, www.aamc
.org/news-insights/how-we-fail-black-patients-pain.

11 CDC, "Infant Mortality Statistics in the United States, 2018: Data from the Period Linked
Birth/Infant Death," *National Vital Statistics Reports* 69, no.7 (July 16, 2020): 9, www.cdc
.gov/nchs/data/nvsr/nvsr69/NVSR-69-7-508.pdf.

12 CDC, "Table A-1a. Age-Adjusted Percentages (with Standard Errors) of Select Circulatory
Diseases Among Adults Aged 18 and Over, by Selected Characteristics: United States, 2018,"
Tables of Summary Health Statistics: National Health Interview Survey, 2018, https://ftp.cdc
.gov/pub/Health_Statistics/NCHS/NHIS/SHS/2018_SHS_Table_A-1.pdf.

13 Neville, Gallardo, and Sue, "Has the United States Really Moved?" 3–21.

14 John Rosales and Tim Walker, "The Racist Beginnings of Standardized Testing," *NEAToday*,
March 20, 2021, www.nea.org/advocating-for-change/new-from-nea/racist-beginnings
-standardized-testing.

15 Rosales and Walker. "Racist Beginnings of Standardized Testing."

16 Rosales and Walker. "Racist Beginnings of Standardized Testing."

17 Chanté Griffin, "How Natural Black Hair at Work Became a Civil Rights Issue," *JSTOR
Daily*, July 3, 2019, https://daily.jstor.org/how-natural-black-hair-at-work-became-a-civil
-rights-issue/.

18 Priya-Alika Elias, "What Does Dressing 'Professionally' Mean for Women of Color?" *Vox*,
March 8, 2018, www.vox.com/2018/3/8/17096202/women-poc-office-dress-code
-professional-attire.

19 Tennille McCray, "Coloring inside the Lines: Finding a Solution for Workplace Colorism
Claims," *Law and Inequality: A Journal of Theory and Practice* 30, no. 1 (2012): 149, https://
scholarship.law.umn.edu/lawineq/vol30/iss1/6.

20 Richard Lee, Harold D. Grotevant, and Wendy Hellerstedt, "Cultural Socialization in Families with Internationally Adopted Children," *Journal of Family Psychology* 20, no. 4 (January
2007): 571–80, https://doi.org./10.1037/0893-3200.20.4.571.

21 Bonilla Silva, Racism without Racists: Colorblind Racism and the Persistence of Racial
Inequality in the United States (New York: Rowman & Littlefield, 2003).

22 Lee et al., "Cultural Socialization in Families," 571–80.

23 Emma Hamilton, Diane R. Samek, Margaret Keyes, Matthew K. McGue, and William G. Iacono, "Identity Development in a Transracial Environment: Racial/Ethnic Minority Adoptees in Minnesota," *Adoption Quarterly* 18, no. 3 (2015): 217–233, https://doi.org/10.1080/10926755.2015.1013593.

24 Deborah Rivas-Drake, Elanor K. Seaton, Carol Markstrom, Stephen Quintana, Moin Syed, Richard M. Lee, Seth J. Schwartz, Adriana J. Umaña-Taylor, Sabine French, and Tiffany Yip, "Ethnic and Racial Identity in Adolescence: Implications for Psychosocial, Academic, and Health Outcomes," *Child Development* 85, no. 1 (2014): 40–57, https://doi.org/10.1111/cdev.12200.

25 EJ Dickson, "Racists Are Worried about the Historical Accuracy of Mermaids," *Rolling Stone*, September 14, 2022, www.rollingstone.com/culture/culture-news/black-little-mermaid-racist-outcry-twitter-1234591724/.

26 Lee and Low Books, "Where Is the Diversity in Publishing? The 2019 Diversity Baseline Survey," *Open Book Blog*, January 28, 2020, https://blog.leeandlow.com/2020/01/28/2019diversitybaselinesurvey/.

27 Richard Jean So and Gus Wezerek, "Just How White Is the Book Industry?" *The New York Times*, December 11, 2020, www.nytimes.com/interactive/2020/12/11/opinion/culture/diversity-publishing-industry.html.

28 Richard M. Lee, "The Transracial Adoption Paradox: History, Research, and Counseling Implications of Cultural Socialization," *The Counseling Psychologist* 31, no. 6 (November 1, 2003): 711–44, https://doi.org/10.1177/0011000003258087.

29 Candice Presseau, Cirleen DeBlaere, and Linh P. Luu, "Discrimination and Mental Health in Adult Transracial Adoptees: Can Parents Foster Preparedness?" *American Journal of Ortho-Psychiatry* 89, no. 2 (2019): 192–200, https://doi.org/10.1037/ort0000385.

30 Sydney K. Morgan and Kimberly J. Langrehr, "Transracially Adoptive Parents' Colorblindness and Discrimination Recognition: Adoption Stigma as Moderator," *Cultural Diversity and Ethnic Minority Psychology* 25, no. 2 (2019): 242–52, https://doi.org/10.1037/cdp0000219.

31 Kevin L. Nadal, Katie E. Griffin, Yinglee Wong, Sahran Hamit, and Morgan Rasmus, "The Impact of Racial Microaggressions on Mental Health: Counseling Implications for Clients of Color," *Journal of Counseling and Development* 92, no. 1 (2014): 57–66, https://doi.org/10.1002/j.1556-6676.2014.00130.x.

32 Nadal et al., "Impact of Racial Microaggressions," 57–66.

33 Nadal et al., "Impact of Racial Microaggressions," 57–66.

34 American Academy of Child and Adolescent Psychiatry, "Children and Racism," *Facts for Families*, no. 135 (March 2021), www.aacap.org/AACAP/Families_and_Youth/Facts_for_Families/FFF-Guide/Children_and_Racism-135.aspx.

35 Hazel Kelly, "5 Things to Know Before You Take a Home DNA Test," California State University, June 22, 2018, www.calstate.edu/csu-system/news/Pages/5-Things-to-Know-Home-DNA-Test.aspx.

36 Kelly, "5 Things to Know."

37 Ellen, Matloff, "If I'm Adopted, Should I Have DNA Testing?" *Forbes*, July 11, 2018, www.forbes.com/sites/ellenmatloff/2018/07/11/im-adopted-should-i-have-dna-testing/?sh=4355ade5e029.

38 Sharon Glennen, "Language Development and Delay in Internationally Adopted Infants and Toddlers: A Review," *American Journal of Speech-Language Pathology* 11, no. 4 (November 2002): 333–39, https://doi.org/10.1044/1058-0360(2002/038).

39 Boris Gindis, "Cognitive, Language, and Educational Issues of Children Adopted from Overseas Orphanages," *Journal of Cognitive Education and Psychology* 4, no. 3 (2005): 291–315, https://doi.org /10.1891/194589505787382720.

40 Glennen, "Language Development and Delay," 333–39.

41 Gindis, "Cognitive, Language, and Educational Issues," 291–315.

42 Glennen, "Language Development and Delay," 333–39.

43 Gindis, "Cognitive, Language, and Educational Issues," 291–315.

44 Monica Pellerone, Alessia Passanisi, and Mario Filippo Paolo Bellomo, "Identity Development, Intelligence Structure, and Interests: A Cross-Sectional Study in a Group of Italian Adolescents During the Decision-Making Process," *Psychological Research and Behavioral Management* 8 (August 20, 2015): 239–249, https://doi.org/10.2147/PRBM.S88631.

45 Melissa Guida-Richards, "Abby Johnson's Video Shows the Problem with White Parents Adopting Children of Color," *ZORA, Medium*, August 28, 2020, https://zora.medium.com /abby-johnsons-video-shows-the-problem-with-white-parents-adopting-children-of-color -949b602e1328.

46 Joshua B. Padilla, Jose H. Vargas, and H. Lyssette Chavez, "Influence of Age on Transracial Foster Adoptions and Its Relation to Ethnic Identity Development," *Adoption Quarterly* 13, no. 1 (April 2, 2010): 50–73, https://doi.org/10.1080/10926751003662598.

47 Padilla, Vargas, and Chavez, "Influence of Age on Transracial Foster Adoptions," 57–73.

48 Raushanah Hud-Aleem and Jacqueline Countryman, "Biracial Identity Development and Recommendations in Therapy," *Psychiatry (Edgmont)* vol. 5, no. 11 (November 2008): 37–44, www.ncbi.nlm.nih.gov/pmc/articles/PMC2695719/.

Chapter 4

1 Oxford Academic, "Understanding Adoption: A Developmental Approach," *Paediatrics and Child Health* 6, no. 5 (2001): 281–91, https://doi.org/10.1093/pch/6.5.281.

2 Stefano Vaglio, "Chemical Communication and Mother-Infant Recognition," *Communicative and Integrative Biology* 2, no. 3 (2009): 279–81, https://doi.org/10.4161/cib.2.3.8227.

3 Lee Dye, "Babies Recognize Mom's Voice from the Womb," ABCNews, January 7, 2006, https://abcnews.go.com/Technology/story?id=97635.

4 Nancy Newton Verrier, *The Primal Wound* (Baltimore: Gateway, 2012).

5 Oxford Academic, "Understanding Adoption," 281–83.

6 Hurley Riley, "The Impact of Parent-Child Separation at the Border," University of Michigan School of Public Health, September 7, 2018, https://sph.umich.edu/pursuit/2018posts/family -separation-US-border.html.

7 Margaret A Keyes, Stephen M. Malone, Anu Sharma, William G. Iacono, and Matt McGue, "Risk of Suicide Attempt in Adopted and Nonadopted Offspring," *Pediatrics* 132, no. 4 (2013): 639–46, https://doi.org/10.1542/peds.2012-3251.

8 Ann E. Bigelow, Michelle Power, Kim MacLean, Doris Gillis, Michelle Ward, Carolyn Taylor, Lindsay Berrigan, and Xu Wang, "Mother–Infant Skin-to-Skin Contact and Mother–Child

Interaction 9 Years Later," *Social Development* 27, no. 4 (June 16, 2018): 937–51, https://doi .org/10.1111/sode.12307.

9 Buffalo Center for Social Research, "What Is Trauma-Informed Care?" University at Buffalo School of Social Work, Accessed October 25, 2022, https://socialwork.buffalo.edu/social -research/institutes-centers/institute-on-trauma-and-trauma-informed-care/what-is-trauma -informed-care.html.

10 NC Division of Social Services, "Trauma-Informed Parenting: What You Should Know," *Views on Foster Care and Adoption in North Carolina: Fostering Perspectives* 18, no. 1 (November 2013), https://fosteringperspectives.org/fpv18n1/know.htm.

11 Melea VanOstrand, "'I'm Not Racist. I Have a Black Family Member!' I'm That Black Family Member. Yes, You Are Racist," *Medium*, August 13, 2020, https://medium.com /@meleavanostrand/im-not-racist-i-have-a-black-family-member-i-m-that-black-family -member-yes-you-are-racist-ba08b0d1e50d.

12 Melissa Guida-Richards, "My Adoptive Parents Hid My Racial Identity from Me for 19 Years," *HuffPost*, February 11, 2021, www.huffpost.com/entry/transracial-adoption -racial-identity_n_5c94f7eae4b01ebeef0e76e6.

13 Nicole Chung, "People Want to Hear That I'm Happy I Was Adopted. It's Not That Simple," *BuzzFeed News*, November 15, 2020, www.buzzfeednews.com/article/nicolechung/being -korean-and-adopted-by-white-parents-nicole-chung.

14 Melissa Guida-Richards, "Abby Johnson's Video Shows the Problem with White Parents Adopting Children of Color," *ZORA, Medium*, August 28, 2020, https://zora.medium.com /abby-johnsons-video-shows-the-problem-with-white-parents-adopting-children-of-color -949b602e1328.

15 Dena @Write-Solutions, comment on Guida-Richards, "Abby Johnson's Video Shows the Problem."

Chapter 5

1 National Institute of Mental Health, "Caring for Your Mental Health," US Department of Health and Human Services, April 2021, www.nimh.nih.gov/health/topics/caring-for -your-mental-health.

2 Head Start Early Childhood Learning and Knowledge Center, "Trauma and Adverse Child-hood Experiences (ACEs)," US Department of Health and Human Services, last reviewed November 22, 2021, https://eclkc.ohs.acf.hhs.gov/publication/trauma-adverse-childhood -experiences-aces.

3 Centers for Disease Control and Prevention, "Fast Facts: Preventing Adverse Childhood Experiences," ICDC: Violence Prevention, last reviewed April 6, 2022, www.cdc.gov /violenceprevention/aces/fastfact.html.

4 Luona Lin, Andrew Nigrinis, Peggy Christidis, and Karen Stamm, *Demographics of the U.S. Psychology Workforce: Findings from the American Community Survey* (Washington, DC: American Psychological Association, July 2015), 8.

5 The information in this section is adapted from Pediatrics: Health Essentials, "Signs That Your Child May Need a Therapist," *Cleveland Clinic*, March 31, 2021, https://health .clevelandclinic.org/signs-your-child-may-need-a-therapist/.

6 Theodora Blanchfield, "What Is Brainspotting Therapy?" *Verywell Mind*, January 7, 2022, www.verywellmind.com/brainspotting-therapy-definition-techniques-and-efficacy-5213947.

7 Theraplay Institute, "What Is Theraplay?" accessed September 27, 2022, https://theraplay .org/what-is-theraplay/.

8 *Psychology Today* Staff, "Internal Family Systems Therapy," *Psychology Today*, last modified May 20, 2022, www.psychologytoday.com/us/therapy-types/internal-family-systems-therapy.

9 Theodora Blanchfield, "What Is Somatic Experiencing Therapy?" *Verywell Mind*, November 2, 2021, www.verywellmind.com/what-is-somatic-experiencing-5204186.

10 Crystal Raypole, "A Guide to Different Types of Therapy," *Healthline*, March 1, 2019, www.healthline.com/health/types-of-therapy#cbt.

11 Raypole, "Types of Therapy."

12 Raypole, "Types of Therapy."

13 Quality Improvement Center for Adoption and Guardianship Support and Preservation, "Dyadic Developmental Psychotherapy (DDP)," *QIC-AG*, accessed September 27, 2022, www.qic-ag.org/logs/dyadic-developmental-psychotherapyddp/.

14 Center for Play Therapy, *What Is Play Therapy?* University of North Texas College of Education, accessed September 27, 2022, https://cpt.unt.edu/what-is-play-therapy.

15 National Institute of Mental Health, "Caring for Your Mental Health."

ACKNOWLEDGMENTS

I was always an avid reader growing up, but until I became an author myself, I didn't realize exactly how much work is involved in the process. From my agent, Kat Kerr from Donald Maass Literary Agency, to my editors Shayna Keyles and Janelle Ludowise, to my copy editor Rebecca Rider and the rest of the staff at North Atlantic Books, I am so incredibly grateful for your help in the production of this workbook from concept to finished product.

As an adoptee, I found strength in community and have been inspired by so many former foster youth, adoptees, birth parents, and even adoptive parents. I would like to specifically thank Marcella Moslow for working with me on this project and for completing the vision I had for a comprehensive workbook that will, hopefully, help many children and parents. I would also like to take the time to thank my friends Danielle Renino and Alissa Jolley for always being there for me and for supporting my work.

I'd like to offer my gratitude to my family and for all they have taught me. To my sons—your humor and courage inspire me to take chances. To my husband—your belief in me and love keep me going. To my mom—your strength to grow and your loyalty to family guides me. To my brother, Rocco—your tenacity and spirit inspire me to keep going. To my sister-in-law, *mi suegra*, and to my father-in-law—you remind me of the beauty and power of family and culture.

For this book in particular, I want to say a special thank-you to my sisters, Sara, Jessica, Paula; to my first mother, Sandra; and to my brothers, Carlos and Juan. Adoption has had a profound impact on our family, and my hope is that more adoptive and foster families can encourage and support connections between families when it is safe to do so. Having you all in my life has been a blessing, and I love you deeply.

ABOUT THE AUTHOR

MELISSA GUIDA-RICHARDS

PHOTO CREDIT: CHARLES RICHARDS II

Melissa Guida-Richards is an adoptee, educator, and advocate based in Pennsylvania. She was adopted in 1993 from Colombia to a family in the US. Her second book, *What White Parents Should Know about Transracial Adoption*, received a starred review from *Publishers Weekly* and was labelled a "must-read for parents who adopt" by *Library Journal*. She has been interviewed live on the *Tamron Hall Show*, *Brut*, *NBCLX*, and *Good Day LA*, has interviews in *The Washington Post* and *People*, and has conducted many workshops with a variety of adoption agencies.

Her viral essay, "My Adoptive Parents Hid My Racial Identity from Me for 19 Years," was published in the *HuffPost* in April 2019. Soon after, she launched the *Adoptee Thoughts* Instagram and podcast to help elevate adoptee voices and educate adoptive parents on the nuances and complexity of adoption.

Guida-Richards graduated from SUNY Fredonia in 2015 with a bachelor of arts in psychology and criminal justice. In addition, she has had work published in *Insider*, the *New York Times*, the *Independent*, *HuffPost*, *Zora* by *Medium*, *Electric Litera-ture*, *EmbraceRace*, and more, and has been on podcasts and radio stations such as NPR's *Code Switch* and *Strange Fruit*, BBC Radio 4, and *Do the Work*. She has also appeared on panels, such as *We the Experts: Adoptee Speaker Series*, *Pretended*, *Heritage Camps*, and more.

You can follow Guida-Richards on Instagram @adoptee_thoughts, listen to her podcast at AdopteeThoughts.com (or any podcast platform), and find all of her work at Guida-Richards.com.

MARCELLA MOSLOW, LCSW, RPT

PHOTO CREDIT: SUE AND MARK KULIGOWSKI

Marcella Moslow is a transracial and transnational adoptee originally from Bogota, Colombia. She has a private practice in Buffalo, New York, that largely consists of adoptees of all ages and their families. Her specializations include early life trauma, attachment, complex trauma, and dissociation, and she is trained and certified in modalities including EMDR (Eye Movement Desensitization and Reprocessing), Progressive Counting, Brainspotting, and Safe and Sound Protocol; she is also extensively trained in play therapy. Moslow is also a trainer, consultant, and educator specializing in the areas of trauma-informed parenting, topics pertaining to adoption and foster care for caregivers and professionals who work with this population, and trauma-informed care within the school system.

You can connect with Moslow @marcellamoslow on Instagram, and she also co-hosts the podcast *Adoptees Dish* (@adopteesdishpodcast), where she discusses the complexities of adoption through a personal and clinical lens.

About North Atlantic Books

North Atlantic Books (NAB) is a 501(c)(3) nonprofit publisher committed to a bold exploration of the relationships between mind, body, spirit, culture, and nature. Founded in 1974, NAB aims to nurture a holistic view of the arts, sciences, humanities, and healing. To make a donation or to learn more about our books, authors, events, and newsletter, please visit www.northatlanticbooks.com.